D1579232

MUSIC
FACTS & TRIVIA

MUSIC
FACTS & TRIVIA

by
Martin Roach

First published in 2004 by
Virgin Books Ltd
Thames Wharf Studios
Rainville Road
London W6 9HA

A catalogue record for this is available from the
British Library.

ISBN 0 7535 09679

Designed by Undertow Design
Typeset by Phoenix Photosetting
Printed and Bound in Great Britain by
Bookmarque Ltd

Author's acknowledgements

Obviously, a book of this nature relies heavily on a vast range of sources. My bibliography points you towards the most important reference works, but in addition I would like to say a big thank you to the following people for their assistance:

Angus Batey, Mark Bedford, Joe Black, Gareth Brown, Kevin Cann, Trish Connolly, Hugh Cornwell, Rob Dimery, John Dingwall, David Gedge, Chuck Grieve, Helen Hartley, Nigel Hassler, Michael Heatley, Wayne Hemingway, Martin James, Ben Johncock, Declan Kyle, Tony McGartland, Jonn Penney, Gary Pettet, Ted Polhemus, David Rowell and Nick White.

Thanks to Darren Haynes for the chart information and research.

Lots of love to Jessica and Harry Dunn.

Special thanks go to Nik Moore for his help with this book and his continued support of my work.

Dedicated to Alfie Blue and Kaye.

Foreword

I once won £25 in a pub quiz because I knew Elvis' Private Roll Number in the US Army. By contrast, I didn't know that the second highest scorer on the TV game show *Pictionary* is the so-called 'ghetto witch-doctor', rapper Coolio. I thought that Chubby Checker wrote 'The Twist', but that was as erroneous as believing that Nero fiddled while Rome burned. I assumed that the violin was invented for classical high society and that jazz was always a sophisticated, critically lauded genre. Wrong again.

If, like me, your mind is a Dyson for the useless – aching under the strain of thousands of snippets of information that you don't have to know, but secretly *need* to – then this book is for you. Having written 82 books on music, youth culture and entertainment since 1991, I thought I knew the odd factoid about music. Think again. Researching this title has been exhausting, silly, demanding, enlightening and, at all times, utterly bonkers. I hope you agree.

Martin Roach
Ridgewell, Essex, June 2004

– trivia –

a piece of information that sits at the back of the cranium, placed there at some indeterminate moment, and lies dormant until the instant in time when a person suddenly doesn't need to know it.

Music Facts and Triva

((•)) The first ever chart listing was actually a 'Top Twelve', released by *New Musical Express* on 14 November 1952. A far cry from the sales-driven computer-compiled mass database of the present day, the first chart was the result of a lengthy stint on the telephone by one Percy Dickens, who personally called a selection of record shops to collate his list. Notably, there were two Number 7s, 8s and 11s.

((•)) Before becoming a granny-baiting Firestarter, The Prodigy's Keith Flint was a road digger.

((•)) In 1980, George Michael was without a record deal and on the dole; in 1990, he was worth £65 million.

((•)) The name of the Beatles-owned company, Apple Corps, set up to manage the band's gargantuan business interests in the late 60s, was a deliberate pun on the words 'apple core'.

((•)) Renowned playwright Israel Horowitz's son is Adam from The Beastie Boys.

((•)) The *Daily Mirror* was the first tabloid to use the phrase 'Beatlemania'.

((•)) Goth legends The Mission acquired such a massive cocaine habit that they actually took to refusing to play unless venues supplied them with a suitably narcotic rider. One live album was even called *No Snow, No Show*.

(•)) One of the great conspiracy theories surrounding The Beatles (of many dozens) was that Paul McCartney was decapitated in a car crash. The story goes that a lookalike was discovered, identical but for a scar under the mouth, and paraded as the real Macc-oy. The rest of the band were said to be hiding clues and messages about the death in their music. The band vehemently denied this rather preposterous conspiracy rumour.

(•)) Freddie Mercury went to boarding school outside Bombay.

(•)) At one point, Freddie Mercury's cocaine and alcohol bills were alleged to have reached £1,000 a week – in the *70s*.

(•)) When Queen were at the top of the 70s charts, most UK fans did not realise that Freddie Mercury was gay. (What?) Same goes for George Michael. (What?)

(•)) Despite Geri Halliwell's solo career being considered a relative 'flop', compared to the commercial might of The Spice Girls, she has nonetheless had more Number 1 singles than Cher, Whitney Houston and Sandie Shaw.

(•)) Paul Anka's huge worldwide hit 'Diana' was released only four months after he won a trip to New York by collecting soup tin labels; on his arrival in the Big Apple he was signed to a record deal aged only sixteen. Anka went on to be musical arranger for Buddy Holly, write lyrics for Sinatra and pen hits for Tom Jones and Donny Osmond.

(•)) When Jerry Nolan, drummer with New York punk act Johnny Thunder and the Heartbreakers, heard the first playback of their 1977 album *L.A.M.F.*, he was so appalled by the sound that he quit the group.

((•)) GG Allin was perhaps one of rock 'n' roll's most shocking performers. His live shows would invariably feature Allin stripping, attacking the audience, cutting himself and/or smearing himself with excrement (take your pick). His music was described by VH-1 as 'unlistenable noise that plumbed the depths of wretched bigotry and hatred'. He frequently threatened to kill himself on stage but eventually died from a heroin overdose. Allin's best known album is called *Freaks, Faggots, Drunks and Junkies*.

((•)) The first Glastonbury Festival in September 1970 offered free milk from dairy farmer/organiser Michael Eavis and was littered with posters that read 'Hippies Keep Out'. Eavis lost £1,500 on that event. The Kinks were paid £500 for their appearance.

((•)) The Boomtown Rats were originally called Mark Skid and the Y-Fronts. Classy.

((•)) Leading instrumentalists in orchestras often snidely call the percussion section 'the kitchen'.

((•)) Mozart was buried in a pauper's grave.

((•)) In 1972 Keith Moon appeared as a nun in a Frank Zappa movie.

((•)) Jim Morrison had become estranged from his family by the time of his premature death.

((•)) Jim Morrison's grave is at Père Lachaise cemetery, also home to the remains of Chopin, Balzac, Oscar Wilde and Edith Piaf. Morrison's headstone had a Greek inscription that translated as 'He was true to his own spirit.'

3

((•)) The first ever million-selling single was Bill Haley And His Comets' '(We're Gonna) Rock Around the Clock'. The song is considered by many to be the very foundation stone of rock 'n' roll. Haley died a heavy drinker and riddled with paranoia, living out his final days in his garage, the walls of which he had painted black. On his death, it was reported that his neighbours were unaware of who he was.

((•)) Rock 'n' roll-loving Teddy Boys caused outrage with their 'anti-social' behaviour, awkwardly dubbed 'the first youthquake'.

((•)) Rockabilly is often reviled as an out-dated style of music and fashion, but in fact it has undergone more rebirths and mutations than most other musical genres, including psychobilly, neo-billy and quiffabilly.

((•)) In America in the 80s, Hong Kong-born Chinese gang members were the last generation to sport the DA and quiff haircut of the rock 'n' roll years.

((•)) In Japan, popular music is sometimes called *zo kugaku*, which translates literally as 'vulgar music'.

((•)) The so-called 'foundation note' of ancient Chinese music was far more than just a note – it was considered to be a cornerstone of the universe and the essence of the human race's well-being. Each dynasty had a different such note (sometimes also called the 'fundamental note') and methods of arriving at it were often bizarre: one process involves laying ninety grains of millet seed end to end and using this distance as a gauge for the length of pipe needed to play the revered note.

(•)) One of the most important solo Chinese instruments is the seven-stringed zither, or *ch'in*, said to date back to the time of Confucius. Philosophers played the *ch'in* and both the instrument itself and those who mastered it were held in the highest esteem. The later Japanese equivalent was the *koto*, a six-foot-long instrument featuring thirteen waxed silk strings.

(•)) The rocking bamboo troughs used to irrigate Indonesian paddy fields are arranged with great expertise so that as they move periodically they create a ghost-like music in the countryside.

(•)) Some South-east Asian tribeswomen pound freshly harvested rice in a musical rhythm.

(•)) South-east Asian xylophones are often fashioned into the shape of peacocks, dragons or sea serpents.

(•)) In 1889, at the Paris International Exhibition centred around the newly erected Eiffel Tower, a Javanese 'gamelan' (meaning 'truck with hammer') orchestra was one of the most popular attractions. One fan was the 27-year-old Claude Debussy.

(•)) The Stray Cats are remembered by many UK music fans as having had a couple of entertaining chart hits in the early 80s ('Runaway Boys', 'Stray Cat Strut'). In fact, frontman Brian Seltzer then travelled extensively through the USA with his own orchestra and became one of that country's biggest live draws, making him a very rich man in the process.

(•)) Chicago-born Jimmy Yancey is credited with inventing 'boogie', a playing style derived from blues and jazz. Some say it is designed to echo the thundering sounds of the railroads and trains that played such a central role in the lives of the suppressed early twentieth-century black population of the southern states.

(◎)) Although most famous for his *Bolero*, Maurice Ravel was fascinated by the emerging jazz and blues genre (at the time jazz horrified the establishment) and he even named one of the movements in his Violin Sonata 'Blues' in its honour.

(◎)) In the 30s and 40s, both Duke Ellington and Count Basie led their respective bands from back behind the keyboards; the prevailing fashion at the time was for the band leader to be front of stage.

(◎)) David Cassidy gave up live performing during his heyday after a fan died at a concert in 1974.

(◎)) The earliest forms of Christian church chants were directly influenced by music performed in Jewish synagogues.

(◎)) In Islam, specially trained singers, named *muezzin*, call worshippers to prayer.

(◎)) During the Crusades of the tenth to twelfth centuries, Christian knights returned from their battles with many Arabic instruments, including stringed items such as the *rebec*. The knights' decision to start marching to Turkish drums is seen by many as the start of the military band's role in the history of combat.

(◎)) The biblical King David is said to have been the first person to formalise religious rituals with music and was said to have been a fine composer and performer himself.

(●) King David also confirmed the men of the tribe of Levi as custodians of the music for the divine service. No relation to Nick Kamen, obviously.

(●) In the very earliest Christian music, song was not considered on a par with the music, which was seen as a very exact and esteemed science. By contrast, hymns and church choirs are integral parts of any religious service today.

(●) The first use of horizontal lines to indicate the relative pitches of certain notes can be attributed accurately to the Italian monk Guido d'Arezzo.

(●) 'Feel-good' music is not an invention of Lycra-clad aerobics teachers. In Greek philosophy, both Aristotle and Plato wrote about the emotional impact of music on the psyche, even attributing certain laws, or *nomoi*, to these feelings.

(●) Madonna's middle name is Louise.

(●) James Last may not be everyone's cup of tea but he has sold 70 million albums. That's a lot of tea.

(●) Quincy Jones' first album was credited to 'Quincy Jones and the All Stars' – one of the latter was star jazz bassist Charlie Mingus.

(●) The very first words recited into a phonograph were spoken by its inventor, Thomas Edison, who said, 'Mary had a little lamb, its fleece was white as snow.' While this fact is widely known, the reaction of his German assistant on hearing those words played back to him is not: 'Gott in Himmel! It have spoke!'

(◈) In 1913 a company called His Master's Voice issued Beethoven's entire Fifth Symphony on eight single-sided primitive records. That company is better known as HMV today.

(◈) Much knowledge of Jewish pre-history has been garnered from the content of the special style of religious chanting known as 'cantillation', an umbrella term actually representing dozens of different colloquial singing styles. Many music historians see cantillation as a unique link between music of the ancient world and European styles.

(◈) In Hebrew cantillation, nothing is written down – everything is memorised. Hand signals help the congregation recall certain ideas or lines.

(◈) In the Bible, the sound created by seven ram's horns (*shofars*), accompanied by a loud cheer from the Israelite army, was used to demolish the walls of Jericho.

(◈) Despite being found dead with signs of a severe beating and gasoline in his digestive system, 60s rocker Bobby Fuller's death was listed as suicide; rumours that he had received threats from mobsters were denied at the time.

(◈) At the age of eighteen, Jimi Hendrix joined the army as part of the magnificently named Screaming Eagles paratrooper squad. He was only demobbed when he broke his ankle on his 26th parachute jump. Thank God that he was.

(◈) Moses was commanded by the Lord to manufacture 'two trumpets of beaten silver'; they were 60 cm long.

(◈) The Bible's biggest music fan, King David, soothed Saul's ailing health and worry by singing and playing instruments to him. The Book of Amos goes further and credits him with the invention of musical instruments.

((•)) Cass Elliot of The Mamas and the Papas died after choking on a ham sandwich… in the same flat where The Who's Keith Moon was to overdose a few years later.

((•)) A bell belongs to the group of instruments called 'idiophones'. But 'wedding bells' sounded better than 'wedding idiophones'. Church bells were originally rung to ward off evil spirits, in contrast to their latterday purpose of calling local people to the service.

((•)) A chordophone is a stringed instrument; an aerophone is a wind instrument; and a membranophone is a term used to describe skinned or membraned instruments. Which makes Keith Moon the greatest membranophone player of all time.

((•)) If DJs are caught short during a live show, they will play either a long song or two back-to-back, known in the trade as 'bathroom records'.

((•)) The Beatles' first Christmas Number 1 was 'I Want to Hold Your Hand'.

((•)) Mercury Records became the first label to stop supplying radio stations with the 'out-dated' format of 78 rpm vinyl, in the spring of 1954.

((•)) The wax 78 rpm disc was replaced by the 7″ disc because it was less fragile. Then vinyl was replaced by CDs, ostensibly because you could spread marmalade on a CD without affecting its performance.

((•)) Bert Williams and his partner were stars of vaudeville and were among the very first black Americans to record on disc. Even though they were black men, they still 'blacked up', with theatre make-up for white lips and eyes, for their performances.

((•)) Time for a sequel? West Indian pianist Winifred Atwell had a million-selling single with 'Let's Have a Party'; suitably buoyed, a year later she released 'Let's Have Another Party'. Her piano cost her £2.50 from a Battersea junk shop.

((•)) Since The Drifters first formed in the early 50s, more than fifty musicians have been in the band's ever-changing line-up.

((•)) At early Tommy Steele gigs, firemen were hired to stand on guard at each side of the stage in case a then unheard-of piece of electrical equipment called 'an amplifier' blew up.

((•)) *Sergeant Pepper's Lonely Hearts Club Band* producer George Martin used only four-track machines to capture The Beatles' masterpiece.

((•)) Guitar legend Les Paul was one of the first people to experiment with multi-tracked recording. In the 40s, he used mono tape recorders, playing along to one track while recording the combined result on another machine.

((•)) Like the violin before it, the guitar's portability has been at the very heart of its popularity. After all, immigrant labour brought in (usually under duress) to the United States were unlikely to make the arduous sea journey from Africa carrying a piano.

(((•))) Early predecessors of the guitar include the lute, the gittern and the *de mano vihuela*.

(((•))) All tape recorders have what is called a 'capstan spindle', which is used to scroll the tape at a constant speed across a 'rubber idler' and the playback heads.

(((•))) The tape in tape machines is a plastic strip coated in metallic oxide, which acts as thousands of tiny magnets to capture the sound. The tape speed is measured in IPS, 'inches per second'. The very first magnetic tape machine was introduced in 1935, and was called the Magnetophone.

(((•))) The word 'bit', used in digital recordings, is drawn from the words 'Binary digIT', which refer to a grouping of binary numbers.

(((•))) A byte is a group of eight bits.

(((•))) Feedback is actually the random noise generated when an original note or chord is amplified and then re-amplified.

(((•))) Possibly the very first electric instrument was La Borde's static electric-driven harpsichord, invented in 1759.

(((•))) The electric piano was invented by Oskar Vierling in 1920.

(((•))) The first commercially viable electric guitar was introduced in 1931 by Adolph Rickenbacker.

(((•))) The guitar's initial huge wave of popularity was not actually during the birth of rock 'n' roll, nor indeed during the genesis of the blues. It was during the reign of Louis XIV, when Italian comedians became regulars at the Royal Court and usually accompanied their routines by strumming on the guitar.

((•)) While elsewhere in Europe the guitar's popularity declined after the court of Louis XIV, in Spain it has always reigned supreme as the national instrument. Germans, by contrast, have no long history of guitar playing in their culture; however, it appears that it was a German instrument maker who crafted the very first six-string guitar, complete with the E, A, D, G, B and E strings that are common currency to this day. Mein Gott.

((•)) The largest live gig ever was not U2 at Wembley; it wasn't Robbie at Slane Castle; nor was it even Simon & Garfunkel in Central Park. It was, arguably, The Chieftains, who performed in front of the Pope and 1.3 million other people at Phoenix Park. Can you hear me at the back?

((•)) Pope Gregory I (of the late fifth century BC) was the man behind the genre known as Gregorian chant.

((•)) A group of notes sung to a single word or syllable, usually to emphasise a crucial moment in a liturgy, is called a 'melisma'.

((•)) A 'misericord' is a carving made into the underside of a pew and was designed to help choirboys rest during long services.

((•)) The friction drum, or 'rommelpot', is not a drum at all but a pot with a stick placed through a membrane covering its open top, from which vibrating noises can be elicited.

((•)) Ravel's *Bolero* – to which Torvill and Dean scored a perfect set of maximums in what is considered ice-skating's greatest ever performance – was originally written to be accompanied by castanets.

((•)) The concluding section of a Roman Catholic mass is titled *Dona Nobis Pacem*, meaning 'God Give us Peace'.

((•)) The word 'gig' may well be derived from the French for jig, namely *gigue*.

((•)) It's a well-known fact that Abba won the Eurovision Song Contest with the song 'Waterloo' in 1974, but this was actually their second attempt at winning, having entered the previous year with 'Ring Ring'.

((•)) By 1978, Abba was earning more foreign currency for Sweden than any other domestic commodity, including Volvo cars. As their English was less than perfect, the band learned all the lyrics phonetically. Despite this linguistic paradox, Abba experts have only spotted one grammatical error in their entire back catalogue, the misuse of the word 'since' in the song 'Fernando'.

((•)) Early Roman and Greek predecessors of the modern-day keyboard used complex systems of water pipes to maintain a supply of air to the instrument. They were a bugger to get on stage, though.

((•)) In theory, the striking of a string to make a hammer hit the keys in a piano means that it should be classed as a 'string' instrument, rather than as a 'percussion' instrument.

((•)) A young boy's voice 'drops' when his larynx toughens, making the pitch his vocal cords create deeper than that of a young girl. The same process is far slower in young girls but this gradual toughening does account for the fact that women's voices are deeper than those of girls.

(◈)) In sacred songs in certain older religions, if a mistake is made during a musical ritual, the piece has to be started all over again to avoid offending the gods.

(◈)) Public hysteria surrounding Teddy Boys exploded on the night of 23 July 1956. Following a high level of youth popularity in the USA, the film *Rock Around the Clock* opened in the UK on that night, at the Trocadero Cinema, in London's Elephant and Castle. In this film, the rock 'n' roll legend Bill Haley and his band The Comets performed the title track, a song they first played in an earlier movie entitled *Blackboard Jungle*. The following day the British press reported that all hell broke loose as soon as the sound of 'Rock Around the Clock' started to boom through the theatre. Ushers and cinema staff had to (allegedly) run for their lives.

(◈)) African hourglass drums, if expertly laced or squeezed with string or rope, can almost exactly mimic the language of the Yoruba tribe in west Africa.

(◈)) Drums are so sacred in African tribal culture that any fugitive taking refuge in a drum house cannot be arrested or even touched until they leave, much in the same way that a church is generally considered a safe house in Western society.

(◈)) Elements of ragtime, the tango, the rumba and the blues can all be traced back to the migrating West African population forcibly shipped to America for slave labour. Similarly, carnivals in both Rio and New Orleans are directly descended from these oppressed people.

(◈)) The so-called *ono* is a secret society of night-hunters in West Africa who only meet during nocturnal hours, plunging through the jungle with fearsome-sounding bull-roarers and pounding drums. This is a tradition continued by Haitian and Caribbean voodoo.

((•)) The Dinka tribe of Sudan have wedding ceremonies that last up to seven days, with almost constant singing and dancing. Imagine the buffet.

((•)) Although the direct inspiration for the film *My Fair Lady* was the 1956 Tony Award-winning Broadway musical by Lerner and Loewe, the original concept goes back to an idea stemming from the 1914 George Bernard Shaw play *Pygmalion*, a far darker piece of work about a woman-hating sculptor whose only true love is his art.

((•)) In the musical *Mary Poppins*, Bert (played by Dick Van Dyke) senses Mary's arrival because there is an easterly wind; she leaves under her flying umbrella on a westerly.

((•)) Richard M Sherman and Robert B Sherman wrote over 35 songs for the musical film *Mary Poppins* in the course of five years' work; inevitably, not every song made it to the final cut. One such 'reject' was 'The Land Of Sand', which was instead used to great effect in *The Jungle Book*, as the hypnotic song 'Trust In Me' by Kaa the snake.

((•)) During the 50s, when many pop hits were mere sanitised covers of notable R&B songs, vocalist Lavern Baker appealed to US Congress to ban the note-for-note re-recording of such classics, or 'cover' versions.

((•)) In May 1955, the US Top Ten singles chart included three versions of 'The Ballad of Davy Crockett' and three versions of 'Unchained Melody', all by different artists. This odd chart multiplicity has never been repeated.

(((•))) One of the very first electronic instrument was the so-called 'Singing Arc'. In 1897, an English scientist by the name of William Duddell was sent to investigate why the new generation of carbon-arc street lights emitted such a continuous whistling sound. He became so enamoured with the noise that he went home and invented a keyboard which created exactly the same sound.

(((•))) The next milestone in electronic music was Thaddeus Cahill's 'Telharmonium', which was exorbitantly expensive to build and weighed no less than 200 tons. Hardly a portable keyboard, then, but in the absence of loudspeakers (yet to be invented), the system was effective at sending music down hotel phone lines for the first time.

(((•))) When the Wurlitzer replaced many small orchestras in the cinema pit for a film's musical accompaniment, in addition to the actual film score many models were able to produce sound effects, such as waves at sea, horses' hooves or even train whistles. Early variations of the concept date as far back as the nineteenth century, one example being the 'Clockwork Polyphon'.

(((•))) The waltz grew out of the Austro-German peasant dance known as a *ländler*.

(((•))) Operetta means 'little opera'.

(((•))) Dr Samuel Johnson called opera 'an exotic and irrational entertainment'. If I paid nearly three hundred quid for a ticket I'd probably think the same.

(((•))) The term 'musical' is actually an abbreviation of 'musical play', which was a genre that originally appeared as light stage entertainment.

((•)) The first Hollywood film of a musical was 1927's *The Jazz Singer*, starring Al Jolson. In it, he uttered the prophetic words, 'You ain't heard nothing yet!'

((•)) In 1983, *In Performance* magazine described the emerging ranks of breakdancers as 'twirling around the axes of their upper bodies like human coffee grinders'.

((•)) In America, break dancing originated from the hardened, street-cool culture of the Bronx and Brooklyn; in the UK, its epicentre was... er, the Wigan Casino.

((•)) The dance style of so-called 'electric boogie' contained body-popping, robotic movements and moonwalking (before Jacko). It was spearheaded by a duo called Shields and Yarnell, who were both pro-fessional mime artists and had studied with Marcel Marceau.

((•)) The ancient Bedouin singing style known as *huda* is designed to mimic the grunt of the camel. That explains a good few of the shock-ers on *Pop Idol...*

((•)) Years before rock 'n' roll upset the parents of the world, the 'King of Swing', Benny Goodman, was reported to have young fans dancing in the aisles during concerts.

((•)) Swing band maestro Glenn Miller played for some time with Ozzie Nelson, father of latterday pop idol Rick Nelson.

((•)) One of the first commercially successful examples of 'cajun' music was Doug Kershaw's 1961 hit 'Louisiana Man'.

(◦)) The Sudanese religious 'dervish' (actually a Persian term meaning 'beggar') dances himself frantically into an actual trance – hence the phrase 'like a whirling dervish'.

(◦)) In the holy month of Ramadan, songs are often sung in the cool and restful evenings after a day's fasting.

(◦)) The rumba originated from a Cuban religious ritual.

(◦)) The word 'conga' means circle, which rather makes a mockery of the drunken party-goers who jump up at the first note of this sound at any wedding reception and form one lone line.

(◦)) Calypso can be traced back to 'griots', local West African musicians who spread gossip and news around a community accompanied by music. The modern-day, less-politicised genre spread from the Caribbean after having arrived there on slave ships.

(◦)) Early calypso singers would sometimes trade insults. Though not directly related, there is a parallel to this in the latterday rap battles between MCs.

(◦)) In the nineteenth century, British colonial forces introduced a law banning calypso on political and moral grounds. It was largely ignored.

(◦)) The easy-going 'soca' rhythms are a combination of soul and calypso, best heard in the work of exponents such as Harry Belafonte.

(◦)) When Trinidadian people wanted affordable instruments to celebrate a festival in the first half of the twentieth century, they used biscuit tin lids and dustbin lids to make drum noises. Within a few years, the ruse had evolved with the help of some oil drums and the steel band became a staple of West Indian life. The highest-pitched drums are known as 'ping-pongs'.

(◉) The son of a grocer, Tony Bennett's surname is actually Benedetto.

(◉) Leonard Cohen is known as 'the Bard of the Bedsits'; Billy Bragg is known as 'the Bard of Barking'.

(◉) Bill Haley was reported to have earned $500,000 from live performances *alone* in 1955.

(◉) 'Rock 'n' roll will be gone by June.'
Variety magazine, early 1955.

(◉) 'Rock 'n' roll is a communicable disease.'
The New York Times, 1956.

(◉) The phrase 'on a wing and a prayer', commonly used in the Western lexicon, was also part of the title for a song, 'Comin' In On A Wing And A Prayer', based on a comment by a US fighter pilot who had barely been able to land his badly damaged aircraft.

(◉) The shortest song to enter the charts was Duane Eddy's 'Some Kind-a Earthquake', lasting only 77 seconds, in 1959.

(◉) By the time Homo sapiens evolved from primates, the species already had the ability to make specific noises through the larynx – as indeed had apes – for a varied number of uses. For males of a breeding age, one of these purposes was to attract females. This was effectively the first example of a human serenade.

(((•))) When Anabella Lwin fronted Malcolm McLaren's big post-Pistols outfit Bow Wow Wow she looked every inch the glamorous, extravagant pseudo-punk and was splashed on the front covers of many magazines, despite being only fourteen when the band started out.

(((•))) Phil Oakey's lop-sided haircut is known as a 'piste' (no, not as in 'taking the...').

(((•))) The first Western pop group to have a record released in China was Wham!. You can almost hear the Republic's leaders saying, 'Told you so...'

(((•))) Passers-by in west London on one night in the winter of 1984 were treated to the surreal sight of Ozzy Osbourne, resplendent in a sequined ball gown, being escorted to the Hammersmith Odeon by Noddy Holder and Don Powell of glam-rockers Slade.

(((•))) At the first ever Jimi Hendrix Convention in Retford, 1984, a Hungarian tribute band called 'Remember Jimi Hendrix' stole the show, complete with their 6' 3" one-legged lead singer.

(((•))) Phillipe Wynne, former lead singer of The Spinners, died on stage at a Californian night club in July 1984.

(((•))) Howard Jones once hired the entire Marquee venue in central London and sent out invites to record companies to come and see him.

(((•))) Culture Club's first single was called 'White Boy' and provocatively displayed Boy George on the sleeve in make-up and dreadlocks.

((•)) Music in ancient times was often associated with magic, and induced trances in the listener – the same has been said about some boy bands.

((•)) It is easier for a very young child to mimic singing than speaking.

((•)) The five-note pentatonic scale still used in many Third World cultures to this day was first recorded in the pre-history of man; the seven-note European form of scales, known as heptatonic, can only be traced back a mere three thousand years.

((•)) The most prominent and popular instrument in tribal Africa remains the drum, whose primary use other than ceremony was communication – large drums are capable of carrying their noise across vast tracts of forest from one community to another. Some drums are tuned to accurately represent the tonal sounds of the language of a particular tribe. These are called 'talking drums'.

((•)) Royal drums in Africa are so sacrosanct that ritualistic sacrifices are often offered when they are being manufactured.

((•)) Both the bushmen and pygmy tribes of equatorial Africa use vocal polyphony that closely resembles west European yodelling.

((•)) 'The Silly Song' in *Snow White and the Seven Dwarfs*, in which the vertically challenged gentlemen entertain their new friend with dancing and song, was actually a replacement for two earlier songs, 'The Lady in the Moon' and You're Never Too Old To Be Young'. The yodellers in the 'Silly Song' were professional session yodellers – not something you come across every day.

(◉) The Disney animated musical *Beauty and the Beast* contains both overt and less obvious references to other films and musicals. At one point, the Beast bears a striking resemblance to Bert Lahr in *The Wizard of Oz*; *Fantasia* is 'winked' at; the hilly vistas of *The Sound of Music* are mimicked; *Frankenstein* is an influence, as is *The King and I*, and *Doctor Zhivago*. Most directly, the animation for the big finale when Belle and the transformed Beast dance together was actually taken from re-drawn animation from a waltz originally created for the 1959 cartoon film *Sleeping Beauty*.

(◉) Thomas Alva Edison has gone down in the history books as the genius who invented the gramophone. Yet in real life he was something of a curiosity figure, known in inventors' circles as 'a tinkerer'. Whatever he was, it wasn't just the record-player that he brought us, but also the storage battery and the electric light bulb. By the time he invented the phonograph – initially to help secretaries dictate memos – he was known as 'The Wizard'.

(◉) Edison's very first phonograph was essentially a cylinder with tin foil wrapped around its circumference.

(◉) In 1877, German Emile Berliner invented a microphone and was rewarded by being offered a job at the Bell Telephone Company. He later also evolved Edison's cylinder phonograph into a machine that could use a flat round disc, or record. His company, The United States Gramophone Company, can be traced through corporate genealogy to elements of EMI, Polygram and RCA Records.

(◉) Remote African tribes have some instruments that are deemed so magical and religious that only a select few are allowed to look at them; there are some known examples of women being punished by death for seeing them.

((·)) Ten thousand kids auditioned to be in the band that became Hear'Say. Only four hundred turned up to try out for The Spice Girls. The advert in *The Stage* magazine for the latter had asked for a new girl group of five 'wannabe starlets'. They apparently came across their name one afternoon in an aerobics class, when a local studio producer called them 'a spicy bunch'.

((·)) The Spice Girls' full names are: Melanie Jayne Chisholm (Sporty 'un), Melanie Janine Brown (Scary 'un), Geraldine 'Geri' Halliwell (Ginger 'un), Victoria Adams (Posh 'un) and Emma Lee Bunton (Baby 'un). These individual nicknames originated from a *Top of the Pops* magazine article on the girls, which featured an explanatory picture of the then-unknown five in a spice rack.

((·)) Geri Halliwell was cruelly dubbed 'Podgy Spice' by the tabloids; it is believed that at the time she was wearing a size eight dress.

((·)) Best not to mess with Baby Spice: her mother Pauline is a martial arts teacher; her father is a milkman. Emma herself is a green belt.

((·)) One of Mel B's nicknames at school was 'pineapple head'; she says that one of her worst memories was being discovered having a pee in an alley.

((·)) Hertfordshire-born Posh Spice's parents made their money in electrical retail. Victoria's parents were so rich that she had to beg them not to pick her up from school in the family Rolls-Royce.

((·)) Speaking in *The Spectator*, Geri Halliwell once said Mrs Thatcher was the 'original Spice girl'. I kid you not.

(◈) Jethro Tull lead singer Ian Anderson was said at one time to walk around Luton with a lampshade on his head.

(◈) Erik Satie's 1893 piano piece *Vexations* consists of only a few bars of music, which are to be repeated 840 times.

(◈) Avant-garde musician John Cage invented the so-called 'prepared piano', which had within its innards elastic bands, screws, erasers, bolts, plastic and drawing pins. Why he went to all that trouble, though, remains a mystery, as his most infamous piece is *4'33" for Henry Flint*, which consists of the pianist sitting at the instrument for exactly that length of time and not touching it.

(◈) Worst question to an audience? Prince, after having changed his name once already to 'The Artist Formerly Known As...' then altered it again to 'Squiggle/Symbol'. At a gig shortly afterwards, he wanted to make his point, so demanded 'What's my name?' only to be met with total silence as several thousand people tried to work out how to pronounce the odd hieroglyph.

(◈) Arthur Lee from the band Love once walked off stage mid-set and went to the supermarket.

(◈) Sky Saxon of cult US band The Seeds listed Top Cat as his hero and even lived in a dustbin himself.

(◈) Shirley Bassey's first hit was a version of 'The Banana Boat Song' in 1957. Few realise that (at the time or writing) she is Britain's most successful female solo chart artist ever.

(◈) In January 1964, Elvis paid $55,000 for Franklin D Roosevelt's presidential yacht, *Potomac*.

(◉) When former Shadows rhythm section Jet Harris and Tony Meehan hit Number 1 with their duo debut 'Diamonds', they displaced The Shadows' own 'Dance On' from the top spot. This in turn bumped former Shadows frontman Cliff Richard down to Number 3 with 'Bachelor Boy'.

(◉) Hollywood's Whiskey A-Go-Go opened in January 1963.

(◉) Veteran DJ Jimmy Savile made his recorded debut with the single 'Ahab The Arab' in July 1962.

(◉) In the early 90s, so-called 'New Jack Swing', one of the last soul movements of the century, lined up witty, sexy vocals from powerful male singers against hip-hop beats and a pure pop sensibility. In return, acts such as En Vogue and Salt-N-Pepa led to a boom of so-called 'New Jill Swing'; the latter even wore condoms pinned to their outfits when promoting the single 'Let's Talk About Sex'. Presumably they didn't use them after they were unpinned, otherwise it would have led to the follow-up 'Let's Talk About Lack of Sleep, Let's Talk About Dirty Diapers'...

(◉) Music hall came to the fore from the loins of so-called 'song-and-supper' halls, where diners would be entertained by a widely varied array of artistes.

(◉) The saucy British seaside postcard first started as a kind of visual equivalent to the then popular music hall bawdiness.

(◉) After the late Lisa 'Left-Eye' Lopez argued with her then boyfriend, Atlanta Falcons football star Andre Rison, in June 1994, she is said to have piled his sneakers in the bath and set fire to them. She'd thought the bath was marble – as it had been when she'd previously burnt a stack of teddy bears after a previous argument. However, it had been replaced with a plastic bath and this time the resulting fire virtually destroyed the $800,000 house.

((•)) Ray Charles, unlike Stevie Wonder, was not blind from birth – glaucoma took his sight when he was only six.

((•)) The fourteenth-century Italian composer Francesco Landini was completely blind but was nonetheless a virtuoso on the organ.

((•)) Bluesman Blind Lemon Jefferson died from exposure during one particularly bitter winter in Chicago, during which some men's moustaches were seen to break off.

((•)) Those giants of songwriting, (Jerry) Leiber and (Mike) Stoller, wrote their first hit – for Charles Brown – while still in their teens.

((•)) John Lennon said he felt Buddy Holly's spectacles made wearing glasses 'cool'.

((•)) Charles Hardin Holley dropped the final 'e' in his surname and altered his first name to Buddy when he signed his first record contract.

((•)) British music hall star Vesta Tilley was a very popular female performer during the First World War. Her act consisted entirely of songs performed in full male persona and army uniform.

((•)) So-called *jongleurs* entertained early medieval high society with music, recitals and other displays of artistic skill. It is from this word that the modern-day term 'juggler' originates.

(((•))) The ceremonial investiture of a new knight of the realm was always accompanied by music, sometimes specifically composed for the occasion.

(((•))) The *Jeu d'Adam*, a Medieval French play containing one thousand lines of prose and song, is considered by most literary historians to be the first theatrical achievement of note. As the spine of the work is the songs, it could even be argued that this was the world's first ever musical.

(((•))) Tori Amos (born Myra Ellen Amos) is the great-granddaughter of a Cherokee native American. Her prodigious piano talents are well documented; on one occasion a six-year-old Tori was being teased by an elder member of the Peabody Conservatory and so turned to her tormentor and said 'Fuck you. I can play Mozart.'

(((•))) After one of her frequent stints playing at a lounge club, Tori Amos offered a lift home to one of the venue's regulars, who then raped her. She attempted to exorcise this severe trauma with the album *Little Earthquakes*. She also helped establish the US organisation RAINN, or 'Rape and Incest National Network', to help victims of such crimes. Small wonder, then, that she has been quoted as saying, 'There's nothing worse than a whiny musician. Make your work, stay committed to your work, stand by your work and shut up.'

(((•))) Nacio Herb Brown, who wrote 'Singin' in the Rain' among many other classics, was formerly a tailor and an estate agent.

(((•))) At the end of Gene Kelly's 'Singin' in the Rain' solo routine, he gives his umbrella to a passer-by, actually an Australian actor by the name of Snub Pollard who himself had made his name in early silent slapstick comedies.

((•)) Aboriginal music – with its grunts, snorts and whistles (I'm not talking about Rolf Harris, by the way) – may seem simplistic to Western ears. However, the tradition is actually extremely complicated and some expert singers are even able to sing two different notes at the same time… which must be handy if you are on a tight budget in the studio. The most successful recorded band to draw heavily on this style is Yotha Yundi.

((•)) Some Aboriginal instruments are made from fish skin and reptile leather.

((•)) A genuine didgeridoo should be made from a single branch of a tree that has *already* been partially hollowed out by termites.

((•)) 'Circular breathing' is an advanced technique by which wind instrument players can take air in through the nose while still playing by breathing through the mouth. In theory, this means they could play for an infinite length of time. Although they still need tea breaks and the like.

((•)) In the musical *Guys and Dolls*, the character Sky Masterson gets his name because he is a risk-taking gambler, the best of them all. At one point, the story is told that he once bet $5,000 on a caterpillar race; another time he bet $10,000 that his temperature would go to 104 degrees. He got so excited it went to 106. The young actor who got the job when this musical was first filmed? Marlon Brando.

((•)) Eliza Doolittle's father Alfred in *My Fair Lady* is a refuse collector, called a dustman back then. However, the actor playing him could not have been further from the nature of his role: Stanley Holloway was a child soprano and later star of English music hall, appearing in scores of films including *Brief Encounter*.

(◉) Dave Grohl, a relative veteran of hardcore bands such as Scream, played his first ever gig with Nirvana at the North Shore Surf Club, Olympia, in October 1990.

(◉) For his *Dangerous* album, Michael Jackson was given a cash advance of $18 million by Sony.

(◉) Right Said Fred made 'I'm Too Sexy' for just £1,500; it was a US number 1 single and was only kept off the top spot in the UK by Bryan Adams' all-conquering record-breaker 'Everything I Do (I Do it for You)'.

(◉) Prior to the American Civil War, vaudeville (the US equivalent of music hall) used white performers 'blacked up' for their roles. After the abolition of slavery, they were duly replaced by genuine black performers, such as the revered MB Curtis All-Star Afro-American Minstrels, who enjoyed huge popularity.

(◉) Historians of music hall trace its origins back to Elizabethan times, possibly an era that could be referred to as four hundred years BG (Before George [Formby]).

(◉) Gian Carlo Menotti's opera *The Telephone* features a girl so obsessed with the device that she insists her boyfriend leave her flat and propose to her from a phone box over the road.

(◉) Chris Bell, troubled songwriter with Big Star, was actually a devout Christian but the conflict this brought him into with his lifestyle – drugs, drink and homosexuality – tortured him. After a disagreement in the studio, he drove his Triumph motorcar into a telephone pole, dying instantly.

(●) Mark Feld, aka Marc Bolan, was in a skiffle band before becoming a mod, then enjoyed a brief career as the recording artist Toby Tyler, before finally becoming a glam rock icon.

(●) The first album by Tyrannosaurus Rex was called *My People Were Fair and Had Sky in Their Hair But Now They're Content to Wear Stars on Their Brows*.

(●) After Russian opera star Feodor Ivanovich Chaliapin spent the night with a woman of ill-repute, he offered her two tickets to his show as payment. When she said she needed bread instead of free admission to an opera, he asked her why she hadn't slept with a baker.

(●) America's so-called 'first important composer', Aaron Copland, was the son of two Russians.

(●) Elvis Costello's real name is Declan Patrick McManus.

(●) Bob Marley's Wailers were originally called The Wailin' Wailers.

(●) Jazz and blues legend Count Basie had a minor pop hit with the theme from the 50s TV series *M Squad*, starring Lee Marvin.

(●) Johnnie Ray's gimmick during his 50s career was to break down in tears on stage, earning him the nicknames 'The Cry Guy' and 'The Prince of Wails' among others.

(●) When The Beatles were ruling the world, Russian authorities belittled their impact and tried to ban their music in certain ways, not least by instructing people that it was 'social poison'; however, by the end of the 60s, there were over two hundred rock groups in Moscow alone, bearing such 'un-Russian' names as Hairy Glass and The Nasty Dogs.

(•)) The Soviet rock star Alla Pugacheva has sold in excess of 150 million records in her career, putting her in the super-league of modern music's biggest stars (No, I hadn't heard of her either.)

(•)) Much is made of so-called 'industrialist music' pioneers such as Einsturzende Neubaten, Throbbing Gristle and Kraftwerk, but in fact as early as 1927, Russian composer Alexander Mossolov was producing orchestral works inspired by, and using sounds from, factories – his *Steel Foundry* piece being the most prominent example.

(•)) Later, in 1948, the two composers Pierre Henry and Pierre Schaeffer recorded everyday sounds such as dustbins, trains and street noises and manipulated these samples into actual compositions such as *Train Music*. They called their invention 'concrete music' or *musique concrète*.

(•)) Composer George Butterworth, a contemporary of Ralph Vaughan Williams and noted folk music expert, died in action at the Somme.

(•)) When The Beatles were recording *Revolver*, Viv Stanshall allegedly put raw meat into Ringo Starr's drums to 'foil the Fabs' sound'.

(•)) Many of the works by Russian composer Dmitri Dmitriyevich Shostakovich are based on the notes that make up the initials of his name.

(◔)) North American Indians who perform in the 'buffalo dance' often wear actual buffalo heads, the insides of which have been scooped out to make a frightening mask.

(◔)) The Pueblo Indians from the parched deserts of the south-western USA have rain-making dances and musical rituals that require the handling of live and highly poisonous rattlesnakes. Other rather unpleasant dances involved impaling oneself on a pole, then dancing to the music while wriggling free of the piercing wound. The rather generic term of 'sun dance' covers many such rituals, some of which can go on for days – hence the 'Sundance Festival'.

(◔)) Jay Kay's band name of Jamiroquai is taken from a Native American tribe known as the Iroquois.

(◔)) Shabba Ranks caused outrage in the UK when he said on Channel Four's show *The Word* that gays should be crucified.

(◔)) The Central Asian shaman recalls the souls of the dead by playing his drum. In the Mediterranean, a similar role is given to so-called 'weepers', who cry, exalt and shout to such spirits.

(◔)) In parts of West Africa, the tinkling of bells is used to mark the exact moment when a departed person's soul enters the netherworld.

(◔)) Sudanese drums are often made out of baobab fruit.

(◔)) The resonating stones of Togo, called lithophones, were one of the very first recognised musical instruments other than the voice and parts of the human body.

(◉) Empty turtle shells, found in Guyana, are predecessors of the modern drum, as is the conch shell used in South America.

(◉) 'Brazilian Bombshell' Carmen Miranda became one of the world's most famous Latin American singing and dancing stars – complete with a full basket of fruit on her head, for some reason.

(◉) Hank Williams' real name was Hiram King Williams.

(◉) In August 1952, Hank Williams was fired from The Grand Ole Opry because of his drinking habits.

(◉) In 1974, militia planning an armed coup in Portugal waited until that country's entry for the Eurovision Song Contest was being beamed live on screen (thus emptying the streets) before secretly sending their tanks in.

(◉) The 1971 album *There's A Riot Goin' On* by Sly and the Family Stone was considered by authorities to be a militant piece of work. Notably, it was one of the very first records to contain the sound of a drum machine.

(◉) The 1968 Eurovision entry from Spain titled 'La La La' used the aforementioned word 'La' 138 times.

(◉) The longest song title ever is oddly enough not by some monstrous prog-rock horror band. 'Would You Rather Be a Colonel With an Eagle On Your Shoulder Or a Private With a Chicken On Your Knee?' published in 1918, comprises 81 letters.

(◉) In the 60s, the BBC would not play any song directly about death, hence the ban on Ricky Valance's 'Tell Laura I Love Her'.

33

(◉) In the early twentieth century, the music hall performer Harry Lauder used to perform songs such s 'I Love A Lassie' and 'Glasgow Belongs To Me' dressed in a kilt and sporran. His huge popularity (in both Scotland and England) is thought by many to have started the cartoon stereotype of the Scotsman.

(◉) Music hall became so popular among the working classes that by 1914, with the outbreak of the First World War, a much more stringent licensing law had to be passed that prevented munitions workers from turning up for work hung-over – or not at all. The genre died out almost overnight (to be replaced with 'Variety').

(◉) From the 50s until the early 80s, the BBC ran a very popular show called *The Good Old Days*, which replicated almost exactly the theatres and acts of early twentieth-century music hall.

(◉) The greatest harmonica player ever, Larry Adler, moved to the UK to live after US authorities accused him of harbouring Communist sympathies.

(◉) The upright piano brought musical instruments into many homes; immediately, demand rose for sheet music of popular and folk songs of the day, previously only passed down orally from generation to generation, leading to the modern-day popular sheet music industry. Charles Harris's 'After The Ball' was the first ever million-selling sheet music. Until the late 50s, the numerous 'charts' available in the UK were calculated on sheet music sales rather than record sales.

(◉) During the McCarthy years, when Senator Joe McCarthy vowed to root out any 'Communists' from US society, most folk singers and songwriters were deemed undesirables, especially those from the vein of the protest song.

((•)) For his 1994 album *The Downward Spiral*, Nine Inch Nails' Trent Reznor chose to complete sessions at 10050 Celio Drive in Los Angeles. This was the notorious house where, nearly 25 years earlier, Charles Manson and his followers had brutally killed Sharon Tate, the pregnant actress wife of Roman Polanski, as well as four other people.

((•)) An early incarnation of Kiss was called Sid Cup Kent.

((•)) After a fruitless day auditioning hopefuls who had answered an advert in *The Village Voice*, Kiss were interrupted by one Paul 'Ace' Frehley, who walked in unannounced with one red sneaker and one orange sneaker, did not introduce himself and simply started playing. The cabbie, former mailman and store clerk was recruited within minutes.

((•)) Kiss's album *Alive!* was later included amongst 800 albums chosen by the Library of Congress to represent great American music history. Blur would later have some of their songs sent onboard the UK-based mission to Mars as an example of the Earth's music culture. The *Beagle II* was lost in space, although reports that this was because they couldn't turn off the bloody radio were unconfirmed.

((•)) Before his untimely death in a plane crash in 1997, John Denver was reported to be in talks with the Russian Space Agency about becoming an astronaut – the price for sending him to the Mir Space Station was said to be $10 million. When New Order had to make a settlement towards a copyright case brought against them by Denver, Steven Morris of that Manc band said it was their contribution towards sending him into space. More recently, Lance Bass of N*Sync has also been trying to become the world's first pop-stronaut.

(◉) The 'Kiss Special Edition Comic Book' is one of Marvel Comics' best-selling editions ever.

(◉) David Lynch asked Trent Reznor of Nine Inch Nails fame to write the soundtrack for his film *The Lost Highway*. Lynch travelled to New Orleans to meet Reznor in a studio, where he verbally described the scenes in the film – using only a script – and then left. Trent produced the score without seeing any footage at all.

(◉) In New Orleans, funeral cortèges are traditionally escorted by a walking jazz band.

(◉) The Greek philosopher Aristotle believed that the sound of a flute could seduce a woman almost without fail. He obviously hadn't heard James Galway.

(◉) Liszt was one of many composers who were inspired by the so-called 'dance of death', a medieval series of pictures showing skeletons prancing around as a representation of the various plagues of those dark years.

(◉) In ancient times, people believed music was made by spirits because it literally 'came out of the air'.

(◉) Fish's real name is Derek Dick. He was right to change it to Fish.

(◉) The first hit song of British origin to contain the word 'rock' in the title was not by Cliff Richard or The Beatles or The Rolling Stones, but by The Goons. Their single 'Bloodnok's Rock 'n' Roll Call' hit Number 3 in the autumn of 1956.

((•)) The Rolling Stones previewed their 1989 album *Steel Wheels* on a boombox in front of five hundred assembled journalists, having arrived at the press conference on a Metro North train boarded at 125th Street. During the tour to promote the album, Mick Jagger joined startled but delighted fans in the parking lot of the Foxboro Stadium in Massachusetts to sing along to 'You Can't Always Get What You Want'.

((•)) The first song to enter the UK charts at Number 1 was Elvis' 'Jailhouse Rock'.

((•)) Family values – Jerry Lee Lewis's UK tour in 1958 was cut short when the media discovered his third wife was also his fourteen-year-old second cousin.

((•)) Jerry Lee Lewis' brother and one of his sons died in car crashes; his other son drowned in an accident in the family swimming pool.

((•)) Having previously acknowledged some drug use, when David Cassidy talked to the UK media in October 1973 about his new album, he said his only vices now were 'biting my nails'.

((•)) Slade's sartorially challenged Dave Hill once broke his left ankle after falling over in his six-inch platform boots at a gig in Liverpool.

((•)) The first run of the musical *Hair* closed on Broadway after 1,729 performances.

((•)) John Lennon once claimed on US TV that his phones were being tapped by US security services.

((•)) Elvis' first ever concerts in New York were in Madison Square Garden in June 1972.

((•)) Kate Bush learnt to play harmonium on an old instrument in her family's barn but eventually it disintegrated due to mice infestation. Ms Bush has toured only *once*, in 1979.

((•)) George Harrison joined Paul McCartney and John Lennon in The Quarrymen the same month that both Michael Jackson and Madonna were born.

((•)) In a 1958 *NME* poll, super-saintly Cliff Richard was feted, despite (or perhaps because of) being berated by conservative groups as 'crude'.

((•)) Emile Ford is listed as the first British-based black male performer to top the UK charts, with the million-selling 'What Do You Want to Make Those Eyes at Me For?' in the autumn of 1959.

((•)) A band called Johnny and the Moondogs reached the final of *Star Search* in 1959 – three of the members were... Beatles.

((•)) In the 1989 film *Catchfire*, the role of an artist who used a buzz-saw for his painting was played by none other than Mr Tambourine Man Bob Dylan.

((•)) After crossing the Red Sea, Aaron's sister Miriam leads a dance of joy and thanksgiving in the Book of Exodus.

((•)) Handel's *Messiah* as well as *Saul, Israel In Egypt* and *Judas Maccabaeus* were all inspired by stories from the Bible; Beethoven, not known for his religious-themed work, wrote one such oratorio, *Christus am Olberge* (literally 'Christ on the mountain of olives').

((·)) Rock 'n' roll was not the first musical genre to be condemned as socially unacceptable – so were jazz, the waltz, the tango and boogie before it.

((·)) The strongest branch of country & western music is the purist 'hillbilly' style, mostly found around the Appalachian mountains, the source of that most recognisable form of dance, the square dance. We only have ourselves to blame – the early settlers from England, Scotland and France started the style. Like ragtime players before them, they also sometimes utilised washboards, this time played with great skill using thimbles on their thumbs. This partly inspired the fleetingly popular skiffle scene of the 50s.

((·)) American composer Henry Cowell came up with the concept of 'tone clusters', which were chords made up of several adjacent notes, often played with the palm of the hand simultaneously on a stretch of piano keys.

((·)) George Gershwin died aged only 39, from a brain tumour.

((·)) The ancient name for a tambourine is a 'tof'.

((·)) The double-reeded Turksih *zurna* is the ancestor of the modern-day oboe.

((·)) Egyptians used hand-shaped 'clappers' to scare birds off crops. These carvings, usually made in ivory, subsequently evolved into an early percussive instrument.

((·)) The Turkish janissary band crescent is also known as a 'jingling johnny'. No comment.

((•)) Michael Crawford – star of countless acclaimed musicals as well as (incredible, isn't it?) *Some Mothers Do 'Ave 'Em* as the dim-witted but lovable Frank Spencer – used to perform under the name of Michael Dumble-Smith. He changed it to Crawford after a biscuit delivery lorry from that famous food firm drove past him one day.

((•)) Judy Garland was born Francis Gumm but changed her name after once being wrongly billed as 'Francis Glumm'.

((•)) Songwriter Ivor Novello, after whom the prestigious writers' awards are named, allegedly spent time in Wormwood Scrubs for 'obtaining petrol unlawfully' during the Second World War.

((•)) The master songwriter Irving Berlin was born into poverty and was working from the age of eight, including a job as a singing waiter.

((•)) The phrase 'Give my regards to Broadway' is not actually the name of a musical as people assume; the actual musical that contained this song was called *Little Johnny Jones*.

((•)) Irving Berlin only played the piano in one key.

((•)) The first DJs probably surfaced in 30s Depression-era USA, when hundreds of small radio stations across America competed to lighten the national spirit.

((•)) In the 30s, big bands surged in popularity thanks to the growth of radio, and would often broadcast live sessions from hotels, presumably because radio stations did not at that time have studios big enough to accommodate them all (and also because any self-respecting hotel had its own big band in situ).

(((•))) Decca didn't just turn down The Beatles. When radio was surging in popularity, for a time they banned any of their artists' records from being played across the airwaves, fearing it would affect sales. Smart thinking.

(((•))) The same day that Decca rejected The Beatles, they signed up Brian Poole and the Tremeloes, a five-piece from Dagenham.

(((•))) One of the forefathers of the modern DJ is Alan Freed. His rasping voice and cavernous knowledge of older music found huge favour among young audiences in Cleveland. Freed's show, *The Moondog Rock 'n' Roll Party*, was sponsored by a local record store and can probably claim to be the world's first youth-oriented radio show.

(((•))) When a DJ or more usually a station receives money from an artist or record company to guarantee a certain amount of plays of a record on their station, it is called 'payola'.

(((•))) The Bob Dylan song 'I'll Keep It With Mine' is about Nico (née Christa Päffgen), who was fleetingly in The Velvet Underground.

(((•))) Notorious BIG's second album, *Life After Death*, charted at Number 1 in the US only three weeks after he was gunned down in a drive-by in Los Angeles.

(((•))) In 1966, Roy Orbison was riding motorbikes with his beloved wife Claudette when she was hit by a truck and killed; only two years later, his home in Nashville caught fire and the two eldest of his three sons perished also.

(◈) Country & western music is full of tales about the harder side of life, though many artists are just commenting on other people's misfortune without having experienced much themselves. Johnny Cash, however, was born in a railroad shack – perhaps the inspiration behind his 1957 hit 'Train of Thought'.

(◈) Johnny Cash was married to June Carter. June was the daughter of Maybelle Addington, who was a member of the The Carter Family, widely recognised as the very 'First Family of Country', way back in the 20s and 30s.

(◈) In the 20s, many major record companies actively and unashamedly marketed their records by black artists and for black audiences as 'race records'.

(◈) Elaine Page had a small part as Caroline Winthrop in *Crossroads*.

(◈) Bobby Darin's standard 'Mack the Knife' was initially banned by some radios for encouraging 'gang warfare'.

(◈) In 1961 the Monkee Davy Jones played Ena Sharples' grandson Colin in *Coronation Street* for one episode only.

(◈) Country singer Glen Campbell was also a renowned session man and played guitar for The Monkees.

(◈) 'Silent Night' was the first composition written specifically to be played in church on a guitar in the early 1800s.

(◈) A travelling musician or music teacher used to be called a 'peripatetic', a term now used for school supply teachers of the subject.

((•)) Mick Jagger and Keith Richard went to the same primary school, then went their separate ways, then met up again on a train. All The Rolling Stones' early hits were covers, including songs by Lennon and McCartney, Chuck Berry and Buddy Holly.

((•)) When The Rolling Stones appeared on *The Ed Sullivan Show* to perform 'Let's Spend the Night Together', Mick Jagger was forced to mumble the song's title lyric after being threatened with censorship.

((•)) Only at the end of a lengthy interview with Duran Duran did the late *Tube* presenter Paula Yates realise that she had been sitting on her mike and no one had heard a thing.

((•)) When big band master Glenn Miller's plane 'disappeared' during the Second World War over the English Channel, it was rumoured – and later acknowledged as a possibility – that the RAF may have shot it down by mistake.

((•)) The name of the boat that overturned and nearly killed Simon Le Bon in 1985 was *Drum*.

((•)) In May 1985, despite having had not one UK hit, the US funk band Maze sold out eight nights at Hammersmith Odeon.

((•)) In one episode of *The Simpsons*, Bart befriends a weird loner who is overweight and ugly but claims to be Michael Jackson. The closing credits do not mention the King of Pop – however, it was Jacko doing the voice over.

((•)) Early bowed instruments that were in some ways the predecessors of the violin et al. were actually played in a vertical position with the bowing hand palm upwards, rather than under the neck with the bowing hand palm downwards.

((•)) At the fateful battle of Roncesvalles, the folk hero figure Roland sounded one of music's most unusual instruments, the oliphant, so called as it was made from an elephant's tusk.

((•)) Kinks guitarist Dave Davies released his first solo album a full thirteen years after his first solo single, 'Death of a Clown'. 'I'm a lazy bastard,' he told the press in 1980.

((•)) At U2's debut London gig, there were only six people in the audience.

((•)) When David Bowie played the Elephant Man in a Broadway play about the dreadfully disfigured John Merrick, rave reviews led to huge crowds amassing afterwards to catch a glimpse of the former Ziggy superstar – leading theatre security to their nightly Elvis-like announcement of 'Mr Bowie has left the building.'

((•)) Two months before he was murdered, John Lennon announced that he had signed a record deal with Geffen, leaving fans eagerly looking forward to his 'comeback'.

((•)) In the fourteenth century, the predecessor of the modern trombone, known as a sackbut, was often played with the cheeks being distended for maximum control and volume. One observer of the time noted, 'this makes the face ugly'.

((•)) It is believed by some scholars that primitive man first learned rhythm from sounds in nature, such as the lapping of water on a shore.

(•)) The mathematician Pythagoras theorised that each of the planets issued a distinctive note while spinning, which together formed a musical scale known as the 'music of the spheres'.

(•)) Before sheet music or written music, melodies were passed on orally through generations via families or teachers.

(•)) Two hymns and a drinking song from the second century BC still exist.

(•)) Star of swing music Charlie Barnet wrote 'We're All Burnt Up' after his band's instruments were destroyed in a fire.

(•)) Before The Beatles made the studio at 3 Abbey Road famous, it had already been operating for nearly forty years, and was frequented by names such as Gracie Fields and Glenn Miller. The Fab Four recorded fifteen of their Number 1s there and at one point the studio was so popular it enjoyed seven Number 1s in just five months.

(•)) When The Red Hot Chili Peppers aped The Beatles' famous zebra crossing record cover – as many bands have been wont to do – the Californian foursome's naked-but-for-a-sock-on-the-cock routine was photographed in broad daylight... only for the photographer to get home and find he had no film in his camera. He phoned the Chilis, who were remarkably philosophical about his mistake and met him there again the next morning in their car on the way to the airport, jumped out, took the snap and flew home.

(•)) More people voted for Will Young and Gareth Gates in the final of *Pop Idol* than for the Conservative Party at the General Election in 2001.

(•)) In former Dead Kennedy Jello Biafra's 1979 San Francisco mayoral campaign, he wrote in his manifesto that if he won, all businessmen would have to wear clown suits. He lost.

(•)) Stiv Bators, former member of US punk band The Dead Boys and veteran of that city's underground scene, died in his sleep; he had been hit by a car while on the way to see his girlfriend in Paris. Refusing any medical help and thinking he was not badly injured he went home and lay down, never to get up again.

(•)) Almost without fail, the final thing that a drummer says before being kicked out of a band is, 'Hey you guys, I've got a few songs we could try.'

(•)) One of the first uses of the word 'polyphonic' was as a means to describe multi-layered vocal African forest music, particularly that of the pygmies and bushmen; its contemporary use is more associated with mobile phone ringtones. The actual word means 'several notes at the same time'.

(•)) Itinerant musicians working for a living in Africa were called *griots*, and would sometimes supplement their act with acrobatics.

(•)) Certain instruments such as the bagpipes, hurdy-gurdy and sitar deliberately use a 'drone' as part of the music they make; for many people, the same could be said of Gareth Gates.

(•)) It is widely believed that African music is one of the earliest musical forms, but in fact there is extensive research to show that Aboriginal music from the world's largest island – Australia – substantially predates any known genres from the African subcontinent.

((•)) In the Lake Victoria region of Africa, the flute is believed to have magical properties and is a key instrument played at many community gatherings.

((•)) In Igor Stravinsky's watershed ballet, *The Rite of Spring*, a young girl dances herself to death at a pagan ritual (later seen by some revisionists as a prediction of the First World War). So shocking and avant garde was the ballet when it premiered in Paris in 1913 that a full-scale riot followed the performance.

((•)) Richard Strauss espoused the theory that when conducting, the right-hand thumb should never need to leave the pocket of the waistcoat.

((•)) Enrico Caruso flew in the face of fashion when recording technology arrived. While his peers scorned the recorded medium as soulless and of no value, he saw the commercial potential and so cut his first record (in 1902). He would go on to make more than £1 million from such recordings. Many of his snobbish colleagues died penniless. Caruso could also eat an entire plate of spaghetti bolognese in one mouthful. Apparently. Although that had nothing to do with his record sales.

((•)) The US pop group America was formed by three dependents of servicemen serving in the UK; one of these, Gerry Beckley, later sang on the soundtrack for *The Simpsons*.

((•)) The Beatles were paid $2,400 for appearing on the *Ed Sullivan Show* in 1964.

((•)) One hundred thousand dollars – reported cost of recording *Sergeant Pepper's Lonely Hearts Club Band*; $1 million – reported

47

cost of recording Fleetwood Mac's *Tusk*; $10 million – reported cost of recording Michael Jackson's *Invincible*.

((•)) Before Michael Jackson's *Thriller* became the biggest selling album of all time, Fleetwood Mac's *Rumours* had held the title.

((•)) In certain photographs, Leonard Cohen looks just like Dustin Hoffman. Trust me.

((•)) At one point, Bruce Springsteen was being dubbed (not by him) 'the next Bob Dylan'.

((•)) Van Morrison has been nicknamed 'The Belfast Cowboy'.

((•)) Before her suicide in 1998, punk icon Wendy O Williams of The Plasmatics had been working as a 'wildlife rehabilitator'.

((•)) Joni Mitchell once went 25 years between appearances on *The Tonight Show With Jay Leno*.

((•)) 'I'm not home because I'm dead.' This was the answer machine message recorded by Nikki Sixx of Mötley Crüe, after recovering from being pronounced DOA following a heroin overdose; despite being pulled back from apparent certain death, he discharged himself from hospital and walked home in a pair of leather underpants, before shooting heroin again.

((•)) In 1981, recordings of the late Patsy Cline and late Jim Reeves were spliced together to make completely new duets by two dead people.

(•) When touring with Dave Grohl's Foo Fighters in 2002, Matt Bellamy of Muse was witness to the ultimate karaoke night. Out on the town with Grohl and his band, they passed a bar where a karaoke Foo song was playing – Grohl ran into the bar and proceeded to take the mic, push the bemused Foo fan out of the way and said, 'This is how it's done!'

(•) Later on that tour, Muse's Chris Wolstenholme nearly died while chewing a tube of Smarties – he accidentally inhaled the round coin-sized plastic cap and starting choking as it lodged in his throat. Only a Heimlich manoeuvre by vocalist Matt saved Muse from being reduced from a three-piece to a duo.

(•) Julie Andrews once wore a badge saying 'Mary Poppins was a junkie'.

(•) The Spice Girls' respective solo careers are often berated but they do show a stark difference in popularity: all Geri's singles have gone Top Ten, with four reaching Number 1, making total sales of nearly two million; Sporty Spice isn't far behind, with six Top Tens, two Number 1s and almost as many total sales; Baby is next, with one Number 1, six Top Tens but more than a million less total sales at only 750,000; then the wooden spoon is a close fight between Scary and Mrs Beckham. Mel B has only had three Top Tens, one Number 1 and only 582,000 solo singles sold. Posh just pips her with four Top Tens, no Number 1s (the only Spice lacking in this department), but just slightly more total singles sold, with 598,000.

(•) In 1964, The Beatles dressed up as binmen for an episode of *Blackpool Night Out* with Mike and Bernie Winters.

((•)) George Michael turned down the offer of playing a waiter in an episode of *Miami Vice*; Sinatra was not so cool – he avidly cameoed as a New York cop on one of his favourite shows, *Magum PI*.

((•)) 'Aulophobia' is the irrational fear of a flute.

((•)) Iconography of the god Krishna shows him playing what is called a 'transverse flute', hoping to charm the milkmaids in the forest of Brindavan.

((•)) In Indian music theory, notes are given specific meanings: for example, 'RE' relates to sharp or harsh feelings, 'DHA' represents solemn moods and 'PA' indicates happiness.

((•)) Expert Indian singers begin to learn the art of hearing and repeating 'microtones' – fractions of a semi-tone – from their very early childhood. Most Western singers, even acclaimed classical performers, cannot do this.

((•)) Classical Indian dance divides the body into two sections: *anga*, which includes the major parts such as head, torso, arms and legs, and *upanga*, which includes the minor parts such as nose, face, fingers, chin and even eyebrows.

((•)) The raga in Indian music – meaning the scale, mode and melody – is the core of that subcontinent's music. Although there are literally hundreds of ragas, in general about 130 different ones are used.

((•)) Fiddle bows in the Middle Ages were very often convex in shape, rather than the straight bow found in their modern-day counterparts.

((•)) Liz Taylor, Barbra Streisand, Cher and George Michael have all owned Harley-Davidson motorcycles.

((•)) There was much consternation in America when Elvis appeared in the film *Roustabout* as a drifter riding across the country – on a Honda motorbike, rather than the two-wheeled equivalent of the Stars and Stripes, a Harley-Davidson.

((•)) Mickie Most became one of the first generation of super-producers when CBS guaranteed him £85,000 in 1964 to work with their acts for the next three years.

((•)) Sandie Shaw won a record contract with Pye when an executive from that label overheard an impromptu performance by her in Adam Faith's dressing room one night.

((•)) Joe Cocker used to be a gas-fitter.

((•)) Amazon tribesmen have perfected the art of singing or chanting with an entire lungful of air, fitting entire musical pieces in before the body's breath has expired.

((•)) The horror of pan pipes was originally a very beautiful form of ancient music thought to have been invented by the Incas of South America. Incas also attributed a gender to each instrument.

((•)) It is a good idea not to share a South America nose-flute, especially if there's a bad bug going round.

((•)) Inuits created a so-called 'mouth music', which contains very complicated noises and rhythms almost indecipherable to those outside their culture. Any arguments between fellow Inuits can often be resolved by singing each side of an icy pool in front of the towns-people.

(◉) A devout early North American religious group called the Shakers took their name from the tendency to spontaneously burst into impromptu dance and song. Like Peter Andre, then.

(◉) In Aztec society, musicians were an elite group and spent years training to perform at the many rituals of human sacrifice that littered this ancient culture. But they were not exempt from punishment – a wrong note carried the death penalty. Talk about murdering a song...

(◉) Aztec ritualistic drums were often filled with the blood of human sacrifices. Likewise, the Aztec 'scraper' was a percussive instrument carved from a human femur with notches along the bone's length, making its sound an eerie rasping rattle.

(◉) In the Americas of the days before Christopher Columbus, most instruments were made from clay, such as whistling pots.

(◉) Sam Cooke often used the pseudonym Barbara Campbell when writing songs – it was his wife's name.

(◉) According to David Pickering's *Companion to Twentieth Century Music*, the first concept album was not the likes of *Sergeant Pepper's Lonely Hearts Club Band* or some god-awful prog-rock effort, but instead Frank Sinatra's 1955 release *In the Wee Small Hours*, on which all the tracks centred around the theme of separated lovers.

(◉) Soul king Sam Cooke's death remains shrouded in uncertainty but it appears that he may have been shot by a motel manageress in error after entering a room by mistake.

(((•))) Rita Coolidge, the woman who inspired Joe Cocker's 'Delta Lady', was the daughter of a Cherokee Indian.

(((•))) When Monty Python wrote the 'Spam' song, the manufacturers of the dubious sandwich meat offered to send them free supplies. They politely declined.

(((•))) Alison Moyet supports Southend United FC; Morrissey supports... er... Man Utd.

(((•))) As well as being one of the most important composers of the nineteenth century, Antonin Dvorak was also a pigeon-fancier and a train spotter. An all-round riveting night out at Chez Dvorak, then.

(((•))) King Louis XIV of France was sufficiently accomplished at ballet for him to appear frequently in performances at his own court. To rave reviews, no doubt.

(((•))) Sacha Distel initially broke through as an acclaimed guitarist; indeed, he was 'France's Best Guitarist' for five consecutive years.

(((•))) It is alleged that when news broke that Lonnie Donegan had undergone a heart operation, share prices in Japan plunged – because the money men in the land of the rising sun had mistakenly translated his name as Ronald Reagan.

(((•))) One theory about Pyotr Ilyich Tchaikovsky's death is that he committed suicide over a failed homosexual relationship.

(((•))) Some African tribes have a fertility ritual in which phallic-shaped flutes are the central instrument used.

(◉)) In China, large gongs used to disperse evil spirits were given names that translated literally as 'Sir Earthquake' and 'Sir Tiger'. Some believers took to bathing in the huge gongs for extra security from the devil.

(◉)) The famous ornament/instrument known as 'The Tipu's Tiger' was a wooden carving of a wild animal mauling a British merchant, to the sound of mechanical growls and howls. It was specially commissioned for the Sultan of Mysore in 1790.

(◉)) French mechanical organs are also known as 'calliopes'.

(◉)) The Wurlitzer Company made electric organs and mechanical self-playing pianos as well as their more famous 'automatic record players'.

(◉)) The largest gamelan gong is 35.5 inches in diameter.

(◉)) Burmese gongs are often suspended between two mythological figures, monsters or legendary people.

(◉)) The Indian Sanskrit word for 'sound' also means 'breath' and 'fire'.

(◉)) The foundation block for ancient Indian music is a book called *Bharata Natya-sastra* written in AD 300 by a mysterious Brahman sage.

(◉)) In Indian music, stringed instruments are known among other terms as *tata*, meaning 'stretched'.

(◉)) The Indian jaltarang is a set of porcelain bowls, filled with varying amounts of water so as to produce individual notes or pitches (said by leading musicologist Alan Blackwood to be the precursor of Benjamin Franklin's so-called glass harmonica). The bowls are played with either a bamboo stick or a wet fingertip. But not while travelling, clearly.

(◉) Tchaikovsky's ballet *Swan Lake*, Carl Maria von Weber's opera *Der Freischutz* and Stravinsky's *The Firebird* are all musical pieces based on themes of the occult. So is the fairy-tale opera *Hansel and Gretel* by Engelbert Humperdinck (no, not the Humpster).

(◉) Russian composer Aleksandr Skryabin died of blood poisoning from a sore on his lip.

(◉) *Ken Johnson and his West Indian Dance Orchestra* was one of ten regular shows that viewers missed because the Second World War broke out that week.

(◉) It is alleged in a court case by a former employee of the Godfather of Soul that James Brown once told her he had 'powerful testicles given to me by the government'.

(◉) When James Brown signed to Federal Records in 1956, he recorded 'Please, Please, Please'; the head of the media group that owned Federal was rumoured to have called the song 'a piece of shit'.

(◉) By the end of the 60s, Motown was the largest black-owned corporation in the USA; Berry Gordy, its founder, saw his first venture – a record shop called 3-D Record Mart – go bust.

(◉) In the summer of 2000, rave reviews were posted in Hong Kong for the visiting Moscow Philharmonic Orchestra – only later did it emerge that the real MPO were actually on tour in France. The duped audience members still clamoured for compensation from the maverick band of Russian classical musicians (who were strapped for cash) despite their previous universal acclaim for the performance.

((•)) In the 1880s, shoemaker Orville Gibson experimented by making a mandolin with a carved, arched top similar to that of a violin – and hence began the rock 'n' roll legend that is Gibson guitars.

((•)) Marlene Dietrich had originally wanted to be a violinist.

((•)) Kate Bush was discovered by Pink Floyd's guitarist Dave Gilmour when she was still at school. Gilmour introduced her to EMI, which led to her debut single aged nineteen – 'Wuthering Heights'.

((•)) P Diddy owns a garage-full of luxury motors, but it is his butler – called Farnsworth Bentley – that is one of his most prized assets, reinforcing his claim to be 'the black Sinatra'.

((•)) When super-loon-trousered MC Hammer's legendary spending spree extended to a swimming pool that was so deep that you needed full scuba diving gear to reach the bottom (yes indeed, u can't touch that) his accountants must have started to worry. With good reason. In 1996 Hammer was declared bankrupt.

((•)) In 1967, Keith Moon set off a gunpowder charge in his drum kit for the finale of a TV appearance, in the process searing Pete Townshend's hair and causing substantial ear damage, as well as badly cutting his own leg with the resulting metal fragments. Thanks.

((•)) The car that Who drummer Keith Moon drove into a Holiday Inn swimming pool in 1968 was a Lincoln.

((•)) Cornershop once allegedly asked an interviewer to clear the tables before they would start talking, 'because spoons freak us out'.

((•)) Herb Alpert appeared as an extra, beating a drum, in Cecil B de Mille's epic film *The Ten Commandments*.

((•)) When The Red Hot Chili Peppers' fractious relationship with their debut album producer, former Gang of Four guitarist Andy Gill, reached rock bottom, they left a human turd in a pizza box on the mixing desk for him on his arrival for the next session.

((•)) Former Duran Duran guitarist Warren Cuccurullo is reported to have sold a range of life-size replica dildos of his own cock. Wild boy.

((•)) When asked by a judge if it was possible to spend £293,000 in one year on fresh flowers (a morsel revealed in Elton John's case against his former accountant), the Rocketman simply replied, 'Yes, I like flowers.'

((•)) David Bowie's coke-addled paranoia is rumoured to have reached such levels that at one point he was keeping his urine in the fridge.

((•)) Bryan Ferry of Roxy Music once sported a long quiff of a mullet length, nicknamed 'an elephant trunk' by fashion experts.

((•)) At a 1993 Lollapollooza appearance, rousing protest rockers Rage Against The Machine sat naked in silence for 25 minutes, refusing to play a note and wearing only gaffer tape on their mouths and the initials P, M, R and C on their chests – a brave act of protest against the conservative Parents' Music Resource Center, who were fighting to censor music.

(◉) Oasis' planned overseas debut, supporting The Verve in Amsterdam, had to be pulled after a 'fracas' on the ferry over from Harwich.

(◉) The definitive Ziggy Stardust hairstyle was cut for David Bowie by Suzy Fussey in February 1972; a hairdresser in a salon near Bowie's house, Suzy had already cut David's wife Angie's hair. Bowie was so impressed he invited Suzy to his home at Haddon Hall to give him the same style. Within months, every teenager in the UK wanted a 'Ziggy cut'.

(◉) Drummers are rock bands' most punctual members – they are always the first to arrive anywhere because they keep speeding up.

(◉) John Denver's father briefly held the world speed record for aircraft in his B-58 bomber in 1961.

(◉) In October 1978, Virgin Records coughed up $50,000 to bail Sid Vicious out of the notorious Rikers Island Prison, where he was awaiting trial for the murder of his girlfriend, Nancy Spungeon. The newly liberated Vicious went to a nightclub, where he argued with and then bottled Patti Smith's brother Todd across the face. He was back in prison that same night, with Virgin's bail money gone forever.

(◉) Kurt Cobain was said to be fascinated by the vomit of fellow West Coast musician Tad Doyle. He said it was 'a work of art' and even wrote a song about it, 'Breed', on Nirvana's album *Nevermind*.

(◉) Elvis once flew 879 miles in his private jet, the *Lisa Marie*, to collect a Denver restaurant's speciality, Fool's Gold Loaf. The super-thick peanut butter/jelly dish was said to contain 4,200 calories.

(•)) Status Quo have enjoyed more weeks in the Top 75 (413) than The Rolling Stones (366).

(•)) ABC released one of their biggest hits, 'When Smokey Sings', after lead singer Martin Fry had won a long battle against cancer.

(•)) The original 'wedge' haircut, beloved of UK soulies in the early 80s and seen on bands such as ABC, was actually originated by celebrity hairstylist Trevor Sorbie.

(•)) The so-called 'hair bands' of 80s heavy metal must be one of rock's biggest self-contradictions: they wore make-up, high heels, tight PVC and leather and spent hours coiffing their hair into massive bouffants; yet they were renowned as hard-living, womanising macho cock rockers. Apparently.

(•)) Siouxsie Sioux of Siouxsie and the Banshees fame was initially called Susan X and was a devoted Roxy Music fan.

(•)) The Hungarian composer Paul Abraham enjoyed huge success as one of the last of a breed capable of writing traditional Viennese operettas. Fleeing to France from a disapproving Nazi regime, Abraham suffered a decline in his fortunes. Friends attempting to trace him had no luck until they eventually found him in a mental hospital in 1956. His most popular song had been 'Today I Feel So Happy' – he died in an asylum in 1960.

(•)) Rod Stewart is renowned for his love of football, but he is also a model railway enthusiast. His stage fright has been so severe that at one show he had to sing two songs from backstage.

(◎)) Although a proud Scot, Rod Stewart was actually born in London.

(◎)) Noel Gallagher claims that if you dig deeply enough, you can hear an undercurrent of Nirvana's 'Smells Like Teen Spirit' in the otherwise Beatles-esque 'Wonderwall'.

(◎)) Maverick record producer Joe Meek was made famous by the Tornados single 'Telstar'; one of the band at the time was future father of Muse singer Matt Bellamy. Perhaps Meek might have seen this coming – he claimed to have spoken with Buddy Holly during seances and eventually killed himself and his landlady with a shotgun on the eighth anniversary of Holly's death.

(◎)) Ray Parker Junior only wrote 'Ghostbusters' because the film's star Dan Aykroyd said he wanted something 'danceable'. The song sold nearly one million copies in the UK alone.

(◎)) Most observers cite Queen's promo clip for 1975's 'Bohemian Rhapsody' as the first ever video (it only cost £5,000); yet in 1921, German composer Oskar Fischinger was filming short abstract movies to accompany his compositions. Mamma mia, there you go.

(◎)) In 1976, Benjamin Britten became the first musician to be granted a life peerage by the Queen. He never really got to enjoy the achievement, as he died that same year.

(◎)) Stuart Goddard, aka Adam Ant, took his pseudonym after noting how an insect-related moniker had worked for The Beatles.

(◎)) There are over sixty chord changes in 'Tie a Yellow Ribbon Round the Old Oak Tree'.

((•)) Marc Almond's single 'A Lover Spurned' is rumoured to have cost as much to record as the average album of the time. It reached Number 29.

((•)) Despite being arguably the ultimate 'album band', Pink Floyd's two pivotal long-players *The Wall* and *Dark Side of the Moon* both failed to hit the top spot. Record company files report that the former record took 1,279 hours to complete.

((•)) Even though New Order's 'Blue Monday' sold over one million copies and remains the biggest-selling 12″ record of all time, they never received a gold or platinum disc for their efforts as their label, Tony Wilson's Factory Records, were not members of the British Phonographic Industry at the time. Wilson had some gold statuettes made up instead.

((•)) The 12″ vinyl was initially produced after DJs complained about the difficulty of handling 7″ records all day under pressure and live on air; of course, the larger format also allowed for longer tracks.

((•)) Although punks hated everything Elvis stood for, most of them shared the fact that, like the King, they had no formal vocal training.

((•)) Angus Young's trademark schoolboy outfit on stage was actually his sister's idea.

((•)) Famed for their glam rock outrageousness, Slade were originally called Ambrose Slade and played as the very first skinhead band.

((•)) Bob The Builder's 'Can We Fix It?' outsold Oasis' 'Wonderwall' by 50,000 copies, selling 1,008,777 copies in all. When Bob The Builder's franchise – including this single – was offered to the

American market, the entire board of one global mega-corporation, including the multi-millionaire chairman, turned up for the meeting in check shirts, dungarees and yellow hard hats.

((•)) Former Boyzone star Ronan Keating gave up a US college athletics career and Olympic aspirations to join the band – although he kept his job at a shoe shop for some time after their career first took off.

((•)) Hear'Say's debut single sold 160,000 copies on its first day of release (going on to become the then fastest-selling single ever); the follow-up sold a tenth of that, just 16,000.

((•)) Ozzie legend Frank Ifield, he of 'Waltzing Matilda' and 'I Remember You' fame, was born in Coventry.

((•)) Some US television channels pulled the Teletubbies video for the smash single 'Teletubbies Say Eh-Oh' after unconfirmed reports that when it came on, some small children had been badly injured trying to hug their televisions, which promptly fell on them.

((•)) The simple and repetitive nature of children's nursery rhymes is designed to reassure the young people with a sense of predictability and therefore security. By contrast, the subject matter of many nursery rhymes is actually pretty frightening: how about bubonic plague ('Here We Go Round the Mulberry Bush'), severe concussion ('It's Raining, It's Pouring'), starving livestock ('This Little Piggy Went to Market') and assassination/physical trauma ('Humpty Dumpty'). It would take more than a cookie and milk to get me to sleep after that lot. Night, night.

((•)) Curtis Mayfield was performing at an outdoor concert in Brooklyn in 1990 when a lighting rig fell on him, paralysing him from the neck down for the rest of his life. During the recording of his last album, *New World Order*, he had to lie down on his back to record all the vocals because this was the only position in which his lungs could gulp enough air to sing.

(•) Super-youthful Musical Youth had to pull out of a tour with Kid Creole in 1982 because their local education authority stated it would interfere too much with their schooling.

(•) Iggy Pop badly sprained his ankle during a US tour in 1982 and was strongly advised to rest. The next day he simply gaffer-taped his damaged joint up and carried on.

(•) Syd Barrett did his first media interview since his almost totally reclusive lifestyle and mental health problems began, when two French journalists simply knocked on the door of his mother's house where he lived in October 1982. They were actually returning some of his clothes they had, for some unexplained reason.

(•) The Rolling Stones caused a degree of wrath among the press when *NME* reported that at their press conference to announce their forthcoming 1982 European tour there were no chairs to sit on.

(•) Acker Bilk attributes his instantly recognisable style of clarinet playing to the loss of two front teeth in a school yard fight and the loss of the tip of his finger in a sledding accident.

(•) Some musicians claim Soft Cell's version of Gloria Jones' northern soul classic 'Tainted Love' is impossible to dance in time to.

(•) Pre-porn-possession-conviction Gary Glitter once spent £6,000 on motorised curtains.

(◉) With his hit 'Don't Give Up on Us' riding high in the charts worldwide, *Starsky and Hutch* star David Soul successfully talked a female fan out of a suicide attempt in the north of England via a phone line in LA, after desperate UK police had called him at home.

(◉) Art Garfunkel has a degree in Art History and a masters degree in Mathematics.

(◉) Art Garfunkel did not write 'Bright Eyes'. Mike Batt did, along with 'The Wombling Song'.

(◉) 'The Humpster' Engelbert Humperdinck has the largest fan club in the world – boasting eight million members. In his early days when he was trying to encourage a mysterious image, Engelbert would often escape fans by climbing out of bathroom windows at venues.

(◉) On the 1961 Harry Belafonte album *Midnight Special*, a local harmonica player used for a session is credited as Blind Boy Grunt. This was Bob Dylan. Two years later, Dylan appeared again as Blind Boy Grunt at Doug Dobell's Jazz Record Shop at 77 Charing Cross Road, in order to play harmonica on a Dick Farina and Eric Von Schmidt recording session taking place at the shop.

(◉) Buffalo Springfield were named after a steamroller they saw resurfacing Fountain Avenue in Los Angeles. When their last album was recorded, the animosity within the group meant that various vocals had to be recorded separately so individual warring members did not have to actually meet up.

(◉) While working as a Playboy bunny girl and other day jobs to support her aspiring music career, Debbie Harry declined a lift from serial killer Ted Bundy.

((•)) Shaggy is a former US marine and veteran of the first Gulf War; somewhat removed, then, from his current status releasing a variant of reggae that he calls 'dog-a-muffin'.

((•)) David Hinds, leader of the seminal British reggae band Steel Pulse, was a dedicated follower of Rastafarian culture and used to sport a huge 'tower' of dreadlocked hair in a vertical column over two feet high. Initially, he had taken to wearing a bowler hat on stage and when his dreadlocks began to be moulded by the black hat, he was inspired to grow the hair tree.

((•)) Tom Jones used to sell vacuum cleaners door-to-door.

((•)) 'Homesick Dusty' was the name Elvis used for himself when sending a telegram to *NME* readers thanking them for making him Number 1. He first appeared on that magazine's front cover in June 1956.

((•)) Celine Dion's sugary sentimental love-fest 'Think Twice' was co-written by Pete Sinfield, a former roadie (and lyricist for King Crimson).

((•)) US rapper Coolio, self-styled 'ghetto witch doctor', achieved the second highest score ever on the American TV show *Pictionary*.

((•)) When The Backstreet Boys released the follow-up to their record-breaking *Millennium* album, the new record, *Black and Blue*, 'only' sold eight million copies – disenchanted executives started talking of a 'flop'. N*Sync's long player *No Strings Attached* sold seven hundred copies a minute – that's eleven *a second* for six working days solid – in the first week of its US release.

(●) *NME* reviewed Fugees' global smash single 'Killing Me Softly' as 'barber shop bollocks… it's best if we just forget it ever happened, eh?' Er, apparently not – weeks later, the same band were featured on the front cover of *NME*, billed as 'The biggest rap band on the planet.'

(●) At the point of the release of its namesake single, none of The Bee Gees had ever been to 'Massachusetts'.

(●) Gareth Gates took a full 25 seconds to say his name at his very first *Pop Idol* audition – TV chiefs had to cut the footage down as it was deemed too long a silence for prime-time TV.

(●) The Beatles' last ever show at The Cavern Club earned them £3,000. The Cavern wasn't a cavern at all. It was a group of cellars and former air-raid shelters.

(●) Two members of US group The Allman Brothers were killed in separate motorcycle accidents: Duane Allman and Berry Oakley.

(●) Greg Allman of the same band divorced two-times-wife Cher twice, in 1977 and then in 1978.

(●) The original video idea for Britney Spears' debut single '(Hit Me Baby) One More Time' was a 'Britney Power Ranger'.

(●) John Lennon's 'Imagine' hit the UK Number 1 spot almost ten years after its initial 1971 release on the album of the same name. The record he signed for his killer Mark Chapman a few hours before he was shot is arguably the most valuable record collectors' vinyl in existence.

((•)) Both 'Relax' and 'Two Tribes' by Frankie Goes To Hollywood were composed on the same night in a disused police cell-cum-rehearsal room.

((•)) Despite dominating the world charts with hits from *Saturday Night Fever* and *Grease* in 1978, less than a year later, a John Travolta compilation of hits from both movies barely scraped into the US Top 200 charts.

((•)) The human ear has a pitch range of about 20Hz to 20,000Hz. 'Middle C' is 261.63Hz.

((•)) Eardrums are membranes only a fraction of a millimetre thick.

((•)) The more rapidly a string vibrates on an instrument, the higher the pitch of the resultant note.

((•)) Tone-deaf people can still enjoy a perfect sense of rhythm.

((•)) Some theories suggest that a human being's innate rhythm is a result of spending nine months in the womb listening to the mother's heartbeat.

((•)) When a TV station shuts down for the evening and plays the test tone, this is actually the purest and simplest form of sound wave, called a sine wave.

((•)) Sound is heard when vibrations or changes in air pressure travel to the ear and move the ear drum.

((•)) Debussy and Ravel were both openly influenced by the Impressionist school of art, as well as symbolist poetry. Debussy's

'Prélude à L'Après-Midi d'un Faune' was directly inspired by a poem by Mallarmé.

((•)) The sonata is split into three essential sections: the exposition, the development and the recapitulation.

((•)) The motet is a short piece of unaccompanied sacred music for three or four voices based around a melody sung by a tenor and most commonly used in the thirteenth century.

((•)) The word 'tenor' derives from the Latin for 'to hold', as originally tenors would hold the 'cantus firmus' vocal part while other parts moved around and above it.

((•)) A *zapateado* is a type of Spanish dance in which the performer stamps his feet in set rhythms – not recommended for dyslexics.

((•)) The first Spanish-language single to top the UK charts was Los Lobos' 'La Bamba' in August 1987.

((•)) ZZ Top have booked seats on the first passenger flight to the moon.

((•)) In 1990, New Kids On The Block earned a pre-tax annual wage of $78 million.

((•)) Ken Dodd – aka Professor Yaffle Chuckabutty, Operatic Tenor and Sausage Knotter – released a single in 1965, 'Tears', that sold more copies than The Beatles' 'Can't Buy Me Love' and any single by Elvis.

(◉) The 1991 hit single '(Everything I Do) I Do It for You' by Bryan Adams was based on a melody that co-writer Michael Kamen had been working on since the 60s. In 1992, a 'cease and desist' order was served on a former Ku Klux Klan member to prevent him from using the tune to soundtrack his campaign for office.

(◉) When Sonny (Salvatore) Bono was killed in a skiing accident in 1998, the world's media hounded Cher, despite the fact they had been separated for 25 years. Sonny had met Cher in a coffee shop and the famous duo's early moniker was Caesar and Cleo. After his own solo career faltered, but before he became a congressman, Sonny had run a restaurant in Los Angeles.

(◉) Cher's actual name is Cherilyn Sarkasian LaPier; she was once posted a fan's ear, cut off by the owner with a knife as a gesture of worship. Just send some damn flowers.

(◉) The ancient Vikings heralded ceremonies and battles with an elongated, slim trumpet known as a *lur*.

(◉) The term baroque means 'rough pearl' in its original Spanish form.

(◉) Antonio Vivaldi was also known as *il prete rosso*, 'the priest with the red hair'. Apart from his ubiquitous *The Four Seasons*, he also wrote forty operas and countless other smaller pieces.

(◉) Johann Sebastian Bach and George Frideric Handel were born in the same year, 1685, within a few hundred miles of each other and were both master composers of their day, but they never met.

(⊙) JS Bach was born into such a dynasty of virtuoso musicians that in parts of Germany the name 'bach' was a commonly used byword for musician.

(⊙) When it was announced that the famous organist Dietrich Buxtehude was going to perform in Germany, one 'fan' walked two hundred miles over several weeks to see him. The fan's name? Johann Sebastian Bach(ache).

(⊙) One in twelve Danish people owns a copy of Aqua's 'Barbie Girl'.

(⊙) Blinded by too much oxygen in his incubator at birth, Stevie Wonder (born Steveland Judkins) also has no sense of smell – lucklessly losing that second sense after a 1973 car crash.

(⊙) Jimi Hendrix's solo recording career lasted less than four years.

(⊙) In 1992, Michael Hutchence had a scuffle with a taxi driver and banged his head on the pavement. Only after many months did he go to see a doctor, by which point he had virtually lost all sense of smell and taste, both of which he never recovered.

(⊙) Will Young was the very last auditionee to be accepted for the final fifty of *Pop Idol*, having spent hours in the 'maybe' room.

(⊙) The biggest-selling UK single ever by an act whose primary profession was not music was the near-two-million-selling 'Unchained Melody' by Robson Green and Jerome Flynn (courtesy of Simon Cowell). This made it the *ninth* best-selling single in history – and it kept Pulp's masterpiece 'Common People' off the top spot.

(•) REM's drummer Bill Berry suffered a brain aneurysm on stage in Switzerland.

(•) Bob Dylan's debut album initially sold just five thousand copies.

(•) Eddie Cochran was killed in a car crash that also badly injured Gene Vincent. Shortly afterwards came his first posthumous release: 'Three Steps to Heaven'.

(•) Lennon and McCartney are said to have penned the discursive lyrics to 'She Loves You' while sitting directly opposite one another on two chairs.

(•) Radio 1 DJ Mike Read did not ban Frankie Goes To Hollywood's 'Relax' – he just pulled it off mid-track. The BBC imposed the actual ban. Yet Beeb DJs John Peel and Kid Jensen had already been playing the song – and had even recorded sessions with the band – a full year earlier.

(•) *Grease* producer Allan Carr initially had Elvis in mind to star in the musical; Fonz actor Henry Winkler declined before Carr recruited a relatively unknown John Travolta.

(•) Louis Armstrong's wife Lil Armstrong was a consummate jazz musician and composer herself; she died at a memorial concert for Louis.

(•) Only four UK singles have sold more than two million copies: Elton John's 'Candle in the Wind 97' (4.86 million); Band Aid's 'Do They Know It's Christmas?' (3.55 million); Queen's 'Bohemian Rhapsody' (2.13 million); and Wings' 'Mull of Kintyre' (2.05 million). The latter single by Wings outsold *any* Beatles single.

(◉)) Paul McCartney is the only artist to enjoy Number 1 success in a quintet, quartet, trio, duo and solo.

(◉)) The Beatles refused to appear on *Desert Island Discs*, although McCartney did so, alone, in later years.

(◉)) The first Brian May heard of 'Bohemian Rhapsody' was when Freddie Mercury invited the band to his flat and told them, 'Now dears, this is where the opera section comes in.'

(◉)) Bob Geldof's initial ambition for his Band Aid project was to raise £72,000 – the final total was over £100 million. For the Live Aid spectacular, British Telecom offered Geldof twenty free phone lines. He wanted one thousand. He won.

(◉)) Live Aid was watched by 1.5 billion people.

(◉)) In 1986 Queen played their 658th and last gig.

(◉)) Of Live Aid, Bob Geldof said his global gig was 'the perfect stage for Freddie [Mercury]. He could ponce about in front of the whole world.'

(◉)) Elton John's Diana tribute was in the Canadian Top Twenty for three *years*. Remember, it was actually a B-side (to John's 'Something About the Way You Look Tonight'). John waived royalties and saw his charitable gesture raise over £20 million. It sold 32 million copies in the first 37 days of release.

(◉)) The original 1974 version of 'Candle In The Wind', written about Marilyn Monroe, only reached Number 11.

(( )) At his knighthood ceremony, Elton John was mistakenly introduced as 'Sir John Elton'.

(( )) The very first *Top of the Pops* in January 1964 opened with The Rolling Stones singing 'I Wanna Be Your Man'.

(( )) 'Mississippi' by Pussycat was the first ever Number 1 by a Dutch act. When you listen to the song, you can see why. Oddly, the music for this saccharine track was actually played by four session musicians who were also in a hard-rock act called Scum.

(( )) *NME* reviewed Rod Stewart's mega-hit 'Sailing'/'Stone Cold Sober' as 'might sound all right if you are drunk'.

(( )) Most people remember Take That as a manufactured boy band who suddenly arrived at the top of the charts; in fact, they had to wait through six singles before their first Number 1, 'Pray'.

(( )) Take That took their name from a headline about Madonna.

(( )) The Royal Scots Dragoon Guards' version of 'Amazing Grace', which was a chart-topper in April 1972, was actually recorded as an afterthought during a session of military studio rehearsals, and was only released after a one-off airing on Radio 2 led to massive public demand for a commercial release.

(( )) The early Romantic German composer Carl Maria von Weber's career came to a premature end when he accidentally drank a glass of nitric acid.

(( )) 'Ave Maria' in its original form was a Latin prayer.

(ω) The words *a cappella*, used to describe singing without voices, means 'as in church'.

(ω) The term *allegro* means 'lively' and is used for reasonably fast pieces; what that has to do with the 70s car the Austin Allegro remains a mystery.

(ω) The word *arpeggio* comes from the Italian for 'harp'. It means to play the notes of a chord one by one in a run, rather than together.

(ω) Eccentric nineteenth-century pianist Adolf Henselt had a severe phobia about playing in public and spent much of his forty years performng compositions by Bach to himself, wearing a red fez, with a copy of the Bible sitting on a music stand next to him and his piano stuffed with feathers.

(ω) Niccolo Paganini was so gifted at the violin that observers announced he must be in league with the devil; a theory reinforced when it emerged he'd had to sell his own instrument to pay off mounting gambling debts.

(ω) Louis Armstrong was nicknamed Satchmo, an abbreviation of 'Satchelmouth', meaning 'a person with a wide mouth'.

(ω) Loletta Holloway's late 70s disco single 'Love Sensation' is one of the most sampled records of all time, most notably heard on the huge dance hit 'Ride On Time', by Black Box. This Italian dance outfit was the brainchild of three studio experts and was fronted by striking French model Katrine (untrue press rumours suggested she was really a man).

((•)) Welsh act Lemon Meringue released a cover version of dance hit 'Ride On Time' called 'Ride On Tea Time'. It failed to chart.

((•)) Billy Joel's performing career started aged four, when he was presented as a child piano prodigy, not unlike Beethoven. But without the frilly shirts.

((•)) Irene Cara's Oscar-winning leg-warmer-tastic single 'Fame' did not reach the UK Number 1 spot until a full two years after the film of the same name was released; the single's success was a direct result of the film's spin-off television series.

((•)) Cliff Richard once held the record for being both the youngest and the oldest performer to achieve a Number 1 – with 'Living Doll' (1959) and 'The Millennium Prayer' (1999).

((•)) The Lycra-clad Tight Fit hit 'The Lion Sleeps Tonight' was a modern version of a former South African hunting song entitled 'Mbube'. It was not the first time this track had charted: both The Weavers in 1952 and folk quintet The Tokens in 1961 enjoyed hits with their own renditions. Karl Denver and Robert John also released successful covers of the track. REM recorded it as a bizarre sister track to their own 'Sidewinder Sleeps Tonight', although they chose not to wear the leopard-skin tights.

((•)) Michael Jackson is not the youngest of the Jackson brothers – that is Randy, three years his junior.

((•)) Lycra-clad, make-up-festooned cartoon rock band Twisted Sister managed to sell out the 3,000-capacity New York Palladium in 1979 despite not having a record deal and never having had radio play.

(◦)) At a US Senate Committee on Commerce, Science and Transportation convened to discuss the content of the lyrics and videos of pop music, witnesses who appeared to testify in front of the panel included John Denver, Twisted Sister's Dee Snider and Frank Zappa. Although all three made highly articulate arguments in favour of free speech, as a result of this committee, the record industry in America agreed to the placement of 'Parental Advisory' stickers.

(◦)) Randy Travis' debut album for Warners cost just $65,000 to produce in 1986 but quickly made that same company $5.2 million. This was one of the first albums of the so-called 'New Country' genre.

(◦)) The video for U2's 'Where the Streets Have No Name' was filmed on The Republic Liquor Store's roof at the intersection of 7th and Main in downtown LA.

(◦)) Don Kirshner, music biz maestro and Monkees producer, was rumoured to have formed the cartoon band The Archies out of a desire to avoid the pitfalls of pop star personality clashes and diva-like demands.

(◦)) Petula Clark's hit 'This is My Song' was written by Charlie Chaplin.

(◦)) Joe Strummer was the son of a second secretary in the British diplomatic service, and he was born in the Turkish city of Ankara. His Clash colleague Topper Headon was fined in 1982 for 'stealing a bus stop'.

(◦)) Jonathan King once released a heavy-metal version of cartoon group The Archies' bubblegum pop hit 'Sugar Sugar', under the band pseudonym Sakkarin.

((•)) During the UK invasion of America's charts in the 60s, US authorities became so concerned about the competition to their homegrown talents that they started refusing work visas for UK acts. In response, when American singer Bobby Vinton applied for a work permit in the UK in June 1965, he was also turned down. Fittingly, the single he had been hoping to promote in Britain was called 'Don't Go Away Mad'.

((•)) John Lennon's first book was called *In His Own Write*.

((•)) In 1965, a US bubblegum manufacturer issued a set of 66 cards of Freddie and the Dreamers which, when placed together as a full set, made a three-foot-square picture of the UK group.

((•)) When The Rolling Stones were hitting paydirt in the mid-60s, they were getting a thousand fan letters a week just in the UK; many of these letters repeatedly enclosed fresh sticks of chewing gum, asking each band member to chew them, rewrap them and return them to the sender.

((•)) Freddie and the Dreamers' Freddie Garrity was thrown through his windscreen in a violent car crash in January 1965 but only suffered a few cuts and bruises.

((•)) Ian Dury and the Blockheads' 'Hit Me with Your Rhythm Stick' knocked Village People's 'YMCA' off the top spot in the UK.

((•)) Ian Dury wrote a musical called *Apples*.

((•)) The very first musical instrument is believed to be a one-note whistle made of reindeer phalanx, considered to be at least twelve thousand years old.

((•)) Another very primitive instrument was the bullroarer, which was whirled around the head on a rope or piece of skin and used to connect those gathered with the souls of parted loved ones.

((•)) One of the first orchestras known to exist is that of King Nebuchadnezzar, who embellished his Babylonian kingdom with a resident group of musicians.

((•)) The composer who wrote the score for the film *Bridge Over the River Kwai* – Sir Malcolm Henry Arnold – also wrote a piece designed to be played on three vacuum cleaners, four rifles, a floor polisher and a full orchestra.

((•)) During the peak of their so-called 'Hit Factory' success, producer dream team Stock, Aitken and Waterman (aka PWL) could boast a track in the Top 40 every week from early 1987 to mid-1990.

((•)) Kylie's debut single 'I Should Be So Lucky' was turned down by all the major record labels of the day.

((•)) Jon Bon Jovi worked at a record company for two years before finding fame with his band. His hair is real.

((•)) Early symphonic music did not boast conductors – the keyboardist's role was to keep the rest of the (back then small) orchestra in line. Rolls of sheet music became the first conductors' precursor to an actual baton, and initially there was a vogue for conducting while facing the audience rather than the musicians. Hugh Cornwell of The Stranglers once did the reverse, facing his drummer for an entire gig, while wearing a raincoat to protect him from the audience's barrage of spit.

(◉) One of opera's greatest 'divas', Jenny Lind (1820–87) at one point was invited to tour the USA by Phineas T Barnum. She was famed for her homely image, so perhaps Barnum was intending to sack his own bearded lady and kill two, er, birds with one stone.

(◉) Charles Gounod was so incensed by one critic's harsh review of his masterwork, *Faust*, that he challenged him to a duel.

(◉) Natalie Imbruglia's first screen exposure was as a child model advertising Coca-Cola and Bubblicious gum. Her global smash hit 'Torn' could boast a production team behind it that included Phil Thornalley (ex-Cure), Nigel Godrich (Radiohead), Mark Goldenberg (Eels) and Mark Plati (David Bowie).

(◉) British rapper MC Merlin was given four months' jail for several charges including burglary in the spring of 1989; at the time, he was featured on The Beatmasters' single 'Who's in the House?'

(◉) After pressure from conservative Christian groups, Pepsi eventually shelved plans to broadcast an advert starring Madonna, which made use of footage from her highly controversial 'Like a Prayer' video. The ad had cost them $8 million.

(◉) In the recording studio for *Bad*, the understandably pressurised follow-up to the biggest selling album ever (*Thriller*, 40 million units and rising), Michael Jackson had a variety of pets with him. Bubbles the chimp was a regular, of course, but so too was his snake Crusher. Bubbles spent most of his time during the 'sessions' riding on the back of the Great Dane owned by engineer Bruce Swedien.

(◉) When The Pet Shop Boys signed a lucrative deal with EMI, singer and former journalist Neil Tennant phoned his mom to tell her the great news. She replied, 'But you're not going to give up your job, are you?'

(•))) Presumably as a direct result of its multi-million-dollar sponsorship of the Jacksons tour in December 1984, Pepsi's market share subsequently overtook Coca-Cola's for the first time in its history.

(•))) When The Cure played in South Africa, a riot led to the death of a hot dog salesman.

(•))) The Damned's Rat Scabies is actually called Chris Miller.

(•))) Former Fleetwood Mac guitarist Peter Green was reported in *NME* to have been admitted to a mental hospital after trying to shoot a messenger delivering a royalty cheque to him.

(•))) When EMI signed The Sex Pistols in October 1976, a spokesman for their new record company said, 'Here at last is a group with a bit of guts for younger people to identify with'; two months later, with twelve of the sixteen venues on the Pistols' debut UK tour cancelling the shows, EMI said they were considering their position 'within the contemporary limits of decency and good taste'; a month later they terminated the Pistols' contract.

(•))) The Damned's Captain Sensible was apparently given the name because, according to Rat Scabies, 'he is so damned stoopid'; Scabies himself got his name from his habit of constant scratching, not helped by hanging a rat from the front of his drum kit (all right, it was plastic).

(•))) Cliff Richard once played a sell-out 25-date tour of Russia. I am not making this up.

((•)) Barry Manilow and Bette Midler used to play as unknowns in steam bath houses.

((•)) MTV was launched on 1 August 1981, and the very first clip was Buggles' 'Video Killed the Radio Star'. The set-up costs were $30 million; to give that some context, in 2004 a twenty-second advert slot during the final episode of *Friends* reportedly cost more than $2 million.

((•)) In the 40s, video jukeboxes were placed in some select US public bars to show black-and-white clips of popular songs.

((•)) Although Queen's 'Bohemian Rhapsody' was indeed a seminal video, lesser known videos such as Captain Beefheart's promotional film for the album *Lick My Decals Off, Baby* came long before.

((•)) Ex-Monkee Mike Nesbitt ran a cable channel called *Pop Clips* years before MTV was launched.

((•)) The Spice Girls had enjoyed several Number 1 hits before they ever played a live gig.

((•)) In 2004, it is estimated the cost of launching a previously unknown new boy band or pop act is approximately £1 million.

((•)) The greatest name for a drummer ever – apart from *The Muppets*' Animal, of course – has to be Showaddywaddy's Antiguan-born Romeo Challenger.

((•)) The man who wrote 'Talk to the Animals' for the original film version of *Doctor Dolittle*, Leslie Bricusse, also wrote Max Bygraves' 1960 Eurovision Song Contest entry, 'My Kind of Girl'.

((•)) Mountain-climbing Nepalese Sherpa priests intersperse their reading of scriptures with the jingling of small bells. Presumably not while they are near the edge...

((•)) The Texan songwriter Townes Van Zandt once said, 'There are only two sorts of song – the blues and zip-pa-dee-doo-dah.'

((•)) Prog rockers were not very good dressers. Fact.

((•)) Jon Lord, keyboard player for Deep Purple, composed the 'Concerto for Group and Orchestra' in 1970.

((•)) Mike Oldfield played every instrument on *Tubular Bells*.

((•)) Although many historians trace the word 'gypsy' back to that people's supposed first home of Egypt, in fact their musical legacy as they have traipsed across the globe makes it appear more likely that they originated in India.

((•)) African 'footed drums' are set on their own two legs, often carved to replicate human limbs, looking rather like a drum on top of half a mannequin.

((•)) Ethiopian plectrums are traditionally made from animal claws.

((•)) Pat Boone is descended from American pioneer Daniel Boone.

((•)) Shakin' Stevens had other items of clothing in his wardrobe apart from denim.

((•)) Sammy Davis Jr used to make light of constant racial harassment he endured by saying he was 'the world's only one-eyed Jewish nigger'.

((•)) The gong that is struck by one Billy Wells at the start of Rank Films was actually made of cardboard.

((•)) Some music historians believe the gong originated from the simple cooking pot – the head of a tribe would strike the pot to announce that food was ready.

((•)) The earliest harp may have been a cannibalised hunting bow. This style of instrument is still used to this day.

((•)) Panpipes, the nightmare instrument of a zillion hotel lobbies worldwide, are actually an instrument of the gods: Apollo played a kithara and Triton a conch. Whether this historical influence can be found on *Heavy Metal's Greatest Panpipe Hits* is debatable.

((•)) In Eastern culture, instruments were often shaped like animals – hence the Japanese fish drum or the Chinese phoenix-shaped mouth organ.

((•)) The Spanish Moors are said by some historians to have inspired elements of British morris dancing – the 'moresca' dance may be a precursor, with its bells-on-legs style. Talk about trying to pass the buck.

((•)) The word 'flamenco' probably derives from the time when the Spanish controlled the region of Flanders in northern France.

((•)) The oldest surviving written records of music are Chinese, a collection of three hundred verses dating back to 1100 BC.

((•)) The twelve fundamental pitches of Chinese art music are called *lu*. At one point, the government laid down in law that this theory had to be taught as an essential subject. Before that, Chinese proverbs state that the dozen *lu* are actually the cries of the mythical phoenix. Similarly, the seven-note ancient Indian scale is historically based around sounds such as an elephant's fanfare and a peacock's cry.

(●) Dandy highwayman Adam Ant, aka Stuart Goddard, is the grandson of a pure gypsy.

(●) Adam and the Ants member Marco Pirroni was in an early incarnation of Siouxsie and the Banshees – as was Sid Vicious.

(●) The original version of The New Seekers' 'I'd Like to Teach the World to Sing' was a bona fide jingle for the Coca-Cola advert that made the song famous. Before it could be commercially released – due to huge public demand – all references to said 'soft drink with vegetable extract' had to be removed.

(●) Survivor wrote 'Eye of the Tiger' for *Rocky III* after being asked to contribute to the film's soundtrack by Sylvester Stallone himself, who was a fan of their big-haired soft-metal second album *Premonition*. I feel like doing a press-up just thinking about it.

(●) Actress and singer Julie Covington, starlet of 'Don't Cry for Me Argentina', initially found fame alongside Rula Lenska in the 1977 TV show *Rock Follies*. Of course, Madonna would later enjoy a Top 5 hit with her own version of this song taken from Alan Parker's film of *Evita*.

(●) Julie Covington later recorded a version of Alice Cooper's 'Only Women Bleed'. Now there's a leap of faith.

(●) Alice Cooper's dad was a minister; it was only appropriate, then, that Cooper named himself after a seventeenth-century witch of that name following an ouija board evening. Cooper is now a scratch golfer feared on the LA club circuit.

((•)) When high-street stores started selling the so-called 'Smiley' logo on T-shirts and handbags, it appeared that they had forgotten – or never realised – that the artwork first surfaced on ecstasy tablets at the height of the underground rave scene.

((•)) The origin of the term 'acid house' is not certain, but one theory suggests it derives from an American term for sampling, 'acid burn'. Another theory is that it was inspired by the 1987 single 'Acid Trax' by the group Phuture. Other people claim it was a misappropriation of the US use of the word (where 'acid' meant to sample) by UK underground maverick Genesis P Orridge. The musical roots are easier to trace – innovations by DJs from Detroit and Chicago, spliced with a lashing of British illicit raves.

((•)) Some early house DJs were rumoured to spike the drinks of the clubbers so that their mind-bending rhythms had maximum impact. Allegedly.

((•)) When record pressing plant owner Larry Sherman was asked to manufacture copies of a new song, the like of which he had never heard before, he was so impressed he set up his own record label to release it: Trax. The song was called 'Fantasy' by Jesse Saunders and Vince Lawrence and is considered by many to be the very first true house record.

((•)) Lovebug Starski's lyric 'to the hip, hop, hippety hop' is regarded by many urban-music historians as the origin of the term hip-hop.

((•)) Shaun Ryder has been widely credited with being the first person to bring ecstasy into the UK, although it was said to have been in circulation in Ibiza as early as 1984.

((•)) Giuseppe Verdi and his second wife, Giuseppina Strepponi, appalled high society when they lived together openly as a couple for a dozen years before finally getting married.

((•)) When soprano Gertrud Bindernagel performed the sequence in Wagner's *Siegfried* where the hero awakens her with a kiss, her jealous husband in the audience was so enraged that he promptly shot her as she left the theatre afterwards.

((•)) Early rider: Wagner's room for composing in Bayreuth was always specially perfumed with expensive scents imported from France, to aid his muse.

((•)) Sinatra had his own brand of Beatlemania – called Swoonatra-mania.

((•)) Aretha Franklin's 1987 album *One Lord, One Faith, One Baptism* was recorded live at her father's church in Detroit. There must have been one helluva collection afterwards.

((•)) In the 30s, the gifted gospel singer Mahalia Jackson gave such lively and extravagant performances that some of the more conservative churches banned her.

((•)) In 1961 Frank Sinatra founded his own record label, Reprise.

((•)) Pink Floyd were still working on 'Another Brick in the Wall (Part 2)' only two weeks before its release date; the schoolchildren heard singing on this track were from Islington Green School.

(•) The ultra-extravagant live show for Pink Floyd's *The Wall* was performed only 29 times. It included 45 tons of props and was a financial loss, but the band met the deficit so fans could see the show.

(•) On its 1972 release, nine-year-old Jimmy Osmond admitted he didn't know where the city was that he sang about in 'Long Haired Lover from Liverpool'.

(•) New Order's 'Blue Monday' is alleged to have been the result of experiments with a new drum machine and LSD. One particular 7″ edit was pressed in a quantity of only 25, most of which are still in bassist Peter Hook's wardrobe.

(•) The theme tune for the 70s police show *Van Der Valk* was based on an old Dutch folk tune.

(•) Elton John once backed Brotherhood of Man as a singer on *Top of the Pops* before he himself became somewhat more successful.

(•) Brotherhood of Man's debut single, 'United We Stand', became a signature tune for the gay liberation movement in 70s America.

(•) Brotherhood of Man's Eurovision winning song 'Save Your Kisses for Me' outsold Abba's own contest winner, 'Waterloo'.

(•) 'Merry Christmas Everybody' was one of the few Slade singles from their heyday *not* to use colloquial Black Country spelling – such as 'Mama Weer All Crazee Now'.

(•) Motown successfully penetrated the white mainstream US market, despite being black-owned and boasting a predominantly black roster. By contrast, its biggest rival of the day, Stax, sold predominantly to a black audience, despite the fact that its founder, Jim Stewart, and many of his session players were white.

((•)) The woman behind the 1962 dance craze hit, 'The Locomotion', Little Eva, was previously Carole King's babysitter.

((•)) Spandau Ballet made their mark in the New Romantic era by emerging on stage wearing rugs.

((•)) The most bootlegged band T-shirt of all time is the simple black-and-white 'Frankie Says…' series inspired by, but usually not paying royalties to, Frankie Goes To Hollywood.

((•)) Novelty hit 'Blue (Da Ba Dee)' contained the word 'blue' 27 times; although mocked for being a lightweight pop song, it was actually about severe depression. All the more odd, then, that at one point in 1999 it was being played somewhere on the radio every 150 seconds.

((•)) In August 2002, worries about the British Army's soldier supplies were relegated to just a slim headline on the front page of the *Sun*, while above was a three-quarter-page picture of Kylie next to the headline 'Kylie In Her Underwear'. Only the previous year, the *Sun* had used its considerable tabloid muscle to announce that Kylie's bum was 'a national obsession'.

((•)) Kylie's mega-smash single 'Can't Get You Out of My Head' was co-written by Cathy Dennis, herself a pop star in the late 80s and early 90s with eleven Top 40 hits including 'Touch Me (All Night Long)'.

((•)) Jarvis Cocker's bum-waving in front of Michael Jackson's self-obsessed Brit Awards performance of 'Earth Song' was not just a prank, it was a protest at Jacko's apparently Christ-like self-representation during the song's rendition.

((•)) The 1989 Brit Awards broadcast has been described by some uncharitable observers as 'the worst televised music show of all time'. At the heart of the disaster were the two presenters, former Page Three model Sam Fox and Fleetwood Mac's towering Mick Fleetwood. However, among the scathing press coverage of the admittedly shambolic programme, it was not widely reported that the autocue was faulty and that neither presenter had a cat in hell's chance of making it through the show without incident.

((•)) In 1989, the UK qualifications for earning a gold record were lowered so that more acts could win one.

((•)) Rod Stewart was outraged when it was rumoured his records were being used by the CIA to relay subliminal messages behind the Iron Curtain.

((•)) Punk shockers Sigue Sigue Sputnik's unreleased 1988 single 'Success' was produced by Stock, Aitken and Waterman. Honest.

((•)) Harry Chapin, known by many as 'the Last Protest Singer', died of a heart attack on his way to a benefit concert. His last protest, then.

((•)) The mother of peerless protest and folk singer Woody Guthrie died from Huntington's chorea, a severe nerve disorder. Subsequently, the young Woody was left with his father, who was crippled with financial woes. Woody was therefore sent to be brought up by his uncle and one of the first things his new surrogate father did was... teach him how to play a guitar. Huntington's chorea killed Woody too, in 1967.

(•) In 1941, Woody Guthrie was commissioned to write a series of songs to celebrate the building of some hydro-electric dams. 'Grand Coulee Dam' and 'Pastures of Plenty' resulted.

(•) Although for a time Woody Guthrie was lauded by the authorities – even recording material for the fawning Library of Congress – his Communist sympathies eventually led to a blanket ban of all his work on US radio.

(•) The 52-page booklet that came with Michael Jackson's *HIStory* album, his first since the first sex-abuse allegations against him surfaced in 1993, contained among other flashes of modesty a list of Jacko's many awards, messages of support from numerous celebrities including Elizabeth Taylor and pictures of Jackson with four separate US presidents.

(•) An early Cliff Richard TV appearance on *Oh Boy!* was lambasted by one critic as a display of 'violent hip-swinging, short-sighted, vulgar antics'.

(•) Cyndi Lauper's first job was that of dog kennel cleaner; Mick Jagger was once a porter at a mental hospital; Ozzy Osbourne once worked in a slaughterhouse.

(•) George Michael was sacked from his job at BHS for not wearing a shirt and tie; Boy George was sacked from shelf-stacking at Tesco after parading around wearing two carrier bags – management described his appearance as 'disturbing'.

(((•))) André Previn started his career playing piano to silent films after school. Music myth has it that during one particularly busy movie, which constantly switched from biblical times to the 1920s, he looked up at the screen to find he was playing 'Twelfth Street Rag' to the crucifixion.

(((•))) Richie Valens suffered from a fear of flying; he died in a plane crash.

(((•))) Guitars were originally variants on the harp, which in its infant days was universally believed to be an instrument of the gods, hence its depiction in the hands of many classical deities. Thousands of years later, someone felt moved to write 'Clapton is God' on the walls of countless London walls. So nothing's changed really.

(((•))) JJ Cale was relatively unknown until Eric Clapton recorded a version of his 'After Midnight', which brought him to a whole new audience. Clapton's 'Cocaine' is another Cale composition.

(((•))) King Thothmes IV of Egypt was buried amid paintings of harpists, pipers and lutenists in the knowledge that his ancestors could bring him back to life at a later date along with this cherished collection of musicians. Sort of like Michael Jackson being buried in his oxygen chamber with his own back catalogue.

(((•))) In the first millennium BC, enemy musicians were still considered esteemed civilians and were never harmed. Non-playing captives would have been skewered in various unpleasant ways, however.

(((•))) Egyptians called music 'joy' or 'gladness' and it was represented in their hieroglyphics as a lotus flower. Although many Egyptian gods were represented as animals, some were portrayed as instruments, such as the god Osiris, said to be represented by a sistrum, an ancient form of rattle.

(◑)) At the historically important archaeological dig known as the Royal Cemetery at Ur in what was ancient Babylon, one of the tombs unearthed contained a mass of musical instruments, with one lyre's strings still being touched by the now skeletal and dusty fingertips of its 2,500-year-old owner. (He was dead, obviously.)

(◑)) In AD 1000, St Dunstan showed people an early version of what became known as an Aeolian harp – a stringed instrument set down in a draughty spot and effectively played by the wind. He said this breezy three-string was *actually* given to him by God.

(◑)) The gospel and operatic technique of squeezing the cartilage at the base of the tongue – known as an epiglottis – to solicit a vibrato sound can be traced back as far as the seventh century BC.

(◑)) The sexually suggestive video for The Spice Girls' second single, 'Say You'll Be There', was just one of many promo clips, band artworks, album sleeves and other miscellaneous inspirations drawn from the unique series of films by Russ Meyer, including *Faster, Pussycat! Kill! Kill!* and *Vixen*.

(◑)) 'I know this man is dangerous and I don't want to see British youngsters hacking out his name on their arms...' You might think this was a reference to Manic Street Preachers guitarist Richey Edwards, who famously carved the legend '4 Real' into his forearm in front of journalist Steve Lamacq in an effort to reinforce his band's message. However, it was actually a critical view of Elvis Presley uttered by an English writer in the aftermath of the release of 'Hound Dog'.

(•) Before Elvis, Colonel Tom Parker managed country singers Hank Snow and Eddy Arnold.

(•) RCA bought out Elvis' contract with Sun Records for around $35,000 in 1955.

(•) For Elvis' 1973 TV special *Elvis: Aloha from Hawaii*, an estimated audience of 1,500,000,000 (1.5 billion) tuned in. At the time, there were said to be only 2.5 billion people on planet Earth.

(•) Chuck D of Public Enemy called rap 'the CNN of young black America'.

(•) After being forced to support an act he thought should be below him on the bill, Jerry Lee Lewis delivered a breath-taking performance, culminating in his pouring lighter fluid over his piano and setting light to it, followed by the words, 'I'd like to see any son of a bitch follow that.'

(•) Sid Vicious was only 22 when he died of a drugs overdose.

(•) The Sex Pistols only released one conventional studio album, *Never Mind the Bollocks*.

(•) Sid Vicious was a big Bowie fan and when he couldn't get his hair to stand up like David's, he put his head in an oven to bake it into place.

(•) While in hospital in early 1978, Sid Vicious said to a photographer, 'My basic nature is going to kill me within six months.' He was wrong, but only by half a year.

(•)) In the 50s, jukeboxes were banned within 'hearing distance' of churches.

(•)) Elvis' mid-1956 tour was undertaken with the proviso that if he moved his lower half at all he would be arrested on obscenity charges, a move later duplicated by some TV shows – most notably *The Ed Sullivan Show* – who chose only to film 'The Pelvis' from the waist up.

(•)) The first parental advisory sticker was a conservative reaction to an album by Prince. It is now considered by many record companies to be a handy marketing tool.

(•)) At the audition to confirm the line-up of Boyzone, Ronan Keating, Keith Duffy, Shane Lynch and Stephen Gately sang George Michael's 'Careless Whisper'.

(•)) Second-week sales of Whigfield's abomination 'Saturday Night' were the highest since 1984's Band Aid record, 'Do They Know It's Christmas?' The track was later covered by both The Smurfs and the doll Sindy, to only marginally less painful effect. For some reason the cover artwork for the single featured a linear gearbox.

(•)) When Jerome Flynn was first contacted by *Pop Idol* judge and master A&R man Simon Cowell about recording a single with Robson Green (his co-star in the hit TV show *Soldier, Soldier*), he was trekking in some remote mountains as part of a back-to-basics pilgrimage. At that point he said no. Sadly, he changed his mind.

(•)) Paul McCartney is rumoured to have shelved plans to release a 'punk' record in 1978 allegedly called 'Boil Crisis'.

((•)) When asked whether women were equal to men, noted lothario Dave Lee Roth of Van Halen said, 'Women are absolutely equal. They just can't lift as much.'

((•)) 'I don't know anything about music. In my line of work you don't have to.'
Elvis Presley

((•)) When Bob Dylan took to using electric guitars and a backing band instead of his previously feted solo acoustic shows, he was jeered and booed by many of his disenchanted audiences.

((•)) Child psychologists were consulted to 'create' a language for the TV characters The Teletubbies and many of their apparently nonsensical utterings closely mirror what the average one- to four-year-old says and understands. The four weirdos from Teletubbyland sold more than one million copies of their debut single 'Teletubbies Say Eh-Oh!', despite some controversy about Tinky Winky's sexual orientation.

((•)) In the 60s, a psychic from south London by the name of Rosemary Brown claimed to be receiving new masterpieces from long-dead composers by speaking to them in the afterlife. The famous names she claimed to have spoken with included Liszt, Bach, Beethoven, Chopin and Stravinsky. She wrote the pieces down and experts pored over the manuscripts. They were sceptical initially – after all, Brown allegedly had no musical knowledge at all. Most classical scholars who studied the works became very uneasy about the apparent quality of the music written down by this utterly unqualified lady, and her claims have never been categorically disproved.

((•)) Ridiculed by anti-easy-listening lobbyists he may be, but in the 50s, Perry Como was the world's highest paid entertainer. Thank God times have changed.

((•)) Vicky Vomit and Stanley Sparkle were pseudonyms that Paul Gadd considered before settling on Gary Glitter. Prior to that, he symbolically 'buried' his previous incarnation Paul Raven by launching a coffin into the River Thames.

((•)) Michael Eavis started the Glastonbury Festival by 'ringing up Colston Hall in Bristol and asking how I could get in touch with pop groups'.

((•)) In 1998, The Beastie Boys' fundraising Tibetan Freedom concert was struck by lightning during the course of the show.

((•)) David Soul of *Starsky and Hutch* fame is of Norwegian descent, born to a Lutheran minister and a professor. He turned down a career as a professional baseball player to start a degree in political science. His early career, prior to the hit 'Don't Give Up On Us Baby', was financed by selling encyclopaedias door to door.

((•)) To promote their fourth album, *Ocean Rain*, Echo and the Bunnymen arranged the so-called 'Crystal Day' – a series of events in and around their hometown of Liverpool, including a boat trip on the Mersey, a bicycle ride around the city, an organ recital at Liverpool Cathedral and a drama from the local Chinese Community Centre… and finally a gig by them at St George's Hall, which had not hosted a performance by a band since… The Beatles.

((•)) Labour Party leader Neil Kinnock appeared in the video and on the picture disc for Tracey Ullman's single 'My Guy'.

((•)) Boy George's notoriety in the mid-80s was as prominent in North America as it was in the UK – a Canadian ice hockey match once came to a standstill when the players and crowd all stood staring at a Boy George lookalike.

((•)) A syllabic vocal performance is one in which each note of melody corresponds with a single syllable of text; by contrast, melismatic vocals are those in which a syllable of text is spread over several notes of melody.

((•)) An African tribe may safely voice their disapproval of a witch doctor through song, but to do so in conversation would have dire consequences.

((•)) Latin American flutes known as *gaitas* are made from the stems of the cactus plant, with mouthpieces fashioned from beeswax.

((•)) The Indians of Central and South America uniquely play the turtle shell by moistening the palm of the hand and rubbing it over the shell to produce an odd squeaking sound.

((•)) Some syllables used in shamamist trance-inducing chants are only recognised when used in that musical form and have no meaning in everyday language.

((•)) Carpathian shepherds produce high and trilling vocal sounds by striking their throat and thorax with the palm of their hands. There are stone reliefs that show Assyrians striking their throats in a similar fashion.

((•)) The original purpose of the yodel was for communication between shepherds in the vast and sometimes dangerous Alps where they worked.

((•)) The science of musical instruments is called organology.

((•)) Before their split on Boxing Day 2001, live giants Steps had sold out more than 120 arenas.

((•)) Steven Tyler and Joe Perry of Aerosmith were dubbed the 'Toxic Twins' because of their legendary capacity for drink and drugs.

((•)) Art Garfunkel frequently walks vast distances – he once trekked across Japan, writing poetry en route. Then there was the time he needed the toilet when he and Paul Simon played Central Park, and found himself in a queue of 500,000…

((•)) Engelbert Humperdinck masterminded the theme tune to *Beavis and Butt-head Do America*, a track called 'Lesbian Seagull'.

((•)) After his heyday as 'King of Calypso', Harry Belafonte became a Unicef ambassador.

((•)) The pork-pie hats worn by Two Tone disciples in the late 70s were also known as 'stingy brims' or 'bluebeat hats'.

((•)) Many people mistakenly believe that Verdi's opera *Aida* was commissioned for the opening of the Suez Canal in 1869. It wasn't.

((•)) The great composer Gustav Mahler was actually better known in his own lifetime as a conductor of high regard, most notably of the Vienna Opera.

((•)) Twelve-tone music is known as 'dodecaphonic'. As opposed to Two Tone music, which is called, er, two tone.

((•)) Debbie Harry, later of Blondie fame, once sang with an unsuccessful 60s hippy band called Wind In The Willows. Blondie's eponymous debut album was on Stock Records, the same label as David Soul. Go figure.

((•)) Dexy's Midnight Runners were named after an amphetamine used in northern soul clubs.

((•)) When Tom Jones released 'Green, Green Grass of Home' in November 1966, Elvis Presley was said to have spent hours phoning radio stations to request the song. Presley adored Jones' baritone-to-tenor voice and used to warm up for his own shows by singing 'Delilah'.

((•)) US jazz pianist Bill Evans was one of the first non-military people to sport a crew cut – a close-cropped style that had previously been the almost exclusive preserve of the army. Singing actor Lee Marvin was also an early convert. Baritone saxophonist Gerry Mulligan also started to cut his own crew cut in the 50s, as he could see his hair was receding.

((•)) The saxophone was invented by a Belgian, the instrument maker Adolphe Sax, circa 1840. He had hoped it would become popular with military bands, but such groups mostly chose to ignore it.

((•)) Charlie Parker, aka Bird, who was regarded as one of the greatest jazz masters of all time, died aged only 35.

((•)) Early jazz horn player Buddy Bolden could be heard playing fourteen miles away on a clear night in New Orleans, according to urban legend.

(◑) During his National Service, Elvis was Private Number US53310761. When he was demobbed, there were two tons of fan mail waiting for him at home.

(◑) 'It's Now or Never' was Elvis Presley's biggest UK single, a Number 1 in November 1960 – the song was a cod-operatic, Americanised version of the 1899 Neapolitan standard 'O Sole Mio', later used in a TV advert to sell ice cream.

(◑) The only time Elvis set foot in the UK was during a transfer at an airport in Scotland.

(◑) Elvis's June 2002 Number 1 hit (billed as Elvis vs JXL) 'A Little Less Conversation' was a remix of an obscure B-side, the first time his estate had allowed such a remix. It sealed a chart gap of 25 years since his previous Number 1.

(◑) Coolio earned his nickname after being ribbed for looking like 'Coolio' Iglesias while working as a forestry fireman.

(◑) The famous military march 'Colonel Bogey' was thought of by its composer Kenneth Alford while playing golf. Having failed to hear another player (a colonel) shout 'Fore!', Alford was only alerted after the colonel proceeded to sing the notes C and A. Incidentally, these notes also became the first two notes of the song, which was duly named after the aforementioned military golfer, hence 'bogey'. (Fans of Dad's Army will know the song in its more popular version, 'Hitler, has only got one ball...')

(◑) The consensus is that the very first all-girl supergroup was The Chantels in 1958, fronted by Arlene Smith, who sang on their hit 'Maybe'.

((•)) The Shangri-Las were one of the first all-white girl groups.

((•)) Boy band manager Lou Perlman previously owned a charter airline company. He would regularly take exorbitantly expensive bookings by New Kids On The Block and began to wonder if he was in the wrong business. He switched professions and duly brought us two of the biggest boy bands in history: The Backstreet Boys and N*Sync.

((•)) On The Beatles' last tour of the US, the pilot of their plane spotted bullet holes along its side – said to have been fired at the Liverpudlians' craft by jealous boyfriends of fans.

((•)) Britney Spears spent longer working as an unsigned, undiscovered act than Travis did.

((•)) All Saints were first formed after a chance meeting between Melanie Blatt's taxi-driver father and Nicole Appleton.

((•)) Wyclef is the son of a preacher; his Fugee colleague Pras is the son of a deacon.

((•)) At the height of their laddette, girl-power world domination, one reporter dubbed The Spice Girls 'Oasis in a Wonderbra'.

((•)) Within eighteen months of signing their first record deal, The Spice Girls were the biggest band on the planet.

((•)) Fred Astaire originally wanted to be a songwriter.

((•)) Frankie Avalon was originally a trumpeter.

((•)) So-called 'bark horns' are used by Amazonian tribes to incarnate evil spirits.

((•)) In Africa and Formosa, the 'healing musician' often uses a flute to deliver supposedly magical rites of recovery to sick villagers – often accompanied by whistles, rattles, disguised voices and loud cries.

((•)) Royal Philharmonic Orchestra conductor Sir Thomas Beecham was a member of the Beecham medicinal products family.

((•)) In the big parade for the musical *The Music Man*, Warner Bros used 76 trombones, 24 clarinets, 30 cornets (not 110 as in the lyric), six piccolos, six French horns, six baritone saxes, six euphoniums, six bassoons, twelve military snare drums, six glockenspiels, six sousaphones and six cymbals. They were insured for a total of $35,000.

((•)) The opening number in the musical *The Music Man* is the song 'Rock Island', which actually uses rhythmic speech to imitate the sound of a train, without orthodox melody. Meredith Willson, the musical's creator, called it 'speak-song'. He used this unusual style (the only rap-industrial track ever?) in the musical *1491*, which was a flop. No bloody wonder.

((•)) In the musical *Hello Dolly!* the six-foot-six-inch music theatre legend Tommy Tune appeared in one of only two musical films he starred in… dwarfing his co-star, one Barbra Streisand.

((•)) Although the set of *Hello Dolly!* was partly consumed by fire in June 1977 (a three-building section was razed in just eighteen minutes), the remainder has since been seen in various other productions and shows, including the 'Dreams' episode of *M*A*S*H* and on several occasions in *NYPD*.

(◉) It is well known that Michael Jackson was badly burnt while filming a commercial for Pepsi. The fire began during the sixth take and one of the first bodyguards to pounce on Jackson and help put out the flames was Miko Brando, son of Marlon. Pepsi paid Jackson $1.5 million damages, which he immediately donated to the hospital that had treated him.

(◉) The only genuine surfer in The Beach Boys was Dennis Wilson; sadly he drowned and was allowed a burial at sea after President Reagan made special arrangements for a ceremony normally reserved for naval personnel.

(◉) Madonna is from Bay City, Michigan.

(◉) The famous artwork for Pink Floyd's *The Wall* album and live shows was by the artist Gerald Scarfe.

(◉) Pat Benatar studied opera.

(◉) The alleged practice of recording subliminal messages advocating suicide that are only audible when a record is played backwards (something metal bands are periodically accused of, never with any legal merit – see Ozzy, Black Sabbath, Judas Priest et al.) is called 'backmasking'.

(◉) Sam Phillips is known for 'discovering' Elvis but he also 'found' Howlin' Wolf, Johnny Cash, Carl Perkins, Roy Orbison and Jerry Lee Lewis, among others.

(◉) The first record on The Beatles' Apple label was 'Hey Jude', released in August 1968.

((•)) Snoop Dogg will be eligible for the Rock And Roll Hall Of Fame in Cleveland, USA, in 2017.

((•)) In the course of just over two minutes, the Human Beinz song 'Nobody But Me' contains the word 'no' one hundred times.

((•)) Celine Dion's 'My Heart Will Go On' was nearly omitted from the final cut of *Titanic* because producer James Cameron initially refused to include any vocal pieces in the film. The version released was actually Dion's first demo.

((•)) The raucous so-called 'barrelhouse' style of playing piano was born out of the need to strike poor quality keys on inferior pianos so loudly that customers in noisy pubs could hear the melody.

((•)) The chart-topping Spanish language version of Jennifer Rush's monster ballad 'The Power of Love' is entitled 'Si Tu Eres Mi Hombre Y Yo Tu Mujer'. Try singing that at a wedding after quaffing more champagne than is decent.

((•)) Maurice Chevalier said he never married so that in the morning he had the choice of which side of the bed to get out of.

((•)) The French poet Charles Baudelaire said that bells 'excavate heaven'.

((•)) European bells contain a large clapper within, which is usually struck by a player pulling on a rope below; Oriental bells, however, have no such clapper but instead are struck on the outside by a hammer.

((•)) 'Long trumpet' players in Islam, often seen at feast celebrations such as those for the New Year, turn in sequence as they play towards the four cardinal points of the compass.

((•)) Chinese emperors would have four musicians playing to them from each of the four compass points of the room – arguably the first ever 'surround-sound'?

((•)) Many old Chinese operas are six hours long. I went to one once in Beijing and am ashamed to say that after only four hours I fell asleep.

((•)) The famous Beijing opera genre usually contains two contrasting styles: the romantic tales called *wen* and the more action-packed battles and stories known as *wu*.

((•)) Some Japanese priests who play the traditional bamboo flute do so with a bucket on their head.

((•)) The elegant Noh theatre of Japan dates back to the fourteenth-century work of an actor-musician duo, Kiyotsugu Kan'ami and his son Motokiyo Zeami. The themes are very similar to Greek tragedies, although the barren sets and masks worn by the actors make this a very unique style of musical theatre. Oddly enough, the main actor is known as *shite*, which seems a bit harsh.

((•)) Japanese puppet theatre used many themes taken from Samurai history, which were usually accompanied by an oriental lute.

((•)) The availability of imported vinyl at Liverpool docks is said by musicologists to have played a major role in that city's fascination with music in the 60s.

(◈) The Beatles' moptop haircut was actually the brainchild of a German model, photographer and occasional hairdresser, Astrid Kirchherr, girlfriend of Stuart Sutcliffe, the so-called fifth Beatle who died of a brain tumour. In Scandinavia the haircut was known as a 'hamlet'.

(◈) An 'axe' in modern music is generally a guitar, but in the 30s this phrase referred to a jazz sax or trumpet.

(◈) The original screenplay for the movie *Bodyguard* – which brought us Whitney Houston's nine-million-selling single 'I Will Always Love You' – was actually written years before with Steve McQueen and Diana Ross in mind.

(◈) Former model Whitney Houston used to sing backing vocals for Chaka Khan.

(◈) Pete Townshend is on record as saying the he finds it 'astounding' that anyone rates his 'simple' guitar playing at all.

(◈) Jim Kerr, lead singer of Simple Minds, is on record as saying he doesn't know what a lot of his band's songs are about.

(◈) While The Doors were working on the song 'The End', an acid-tripping Jim Morrison started mumbling, 'Fuck the mother, kill the father'. The song made it on to the album *The Doors*.

(◈) Some fanatical followers of Doors singer Jim Morrison thought his flowing locks were actually proof of his being a modern-day Samson and dreaded the day he might decide to cut them off.

(◈) The year 1968 was one of the biggest years for the afro cut – Sly

Stone toured the US and UK with magnificent examples of the hairstyle and James Brown even changed his conk cut to an afro. The poster of Marsha Hunt's massive afro for the musical *Hair!* increased the popularity of the style still further.

(•)) Led Zeppelin's long-haired appearance made many older music biz executives doubt they were serious about their band. On the contrary, the rockers they snidely dubbed 'hippy-satans' were consummate businessmen and very quickly became some of the richest stars in the world.

(•)) Jimmy Page was hired as a session guitarist for Roy Harper, Michael Chapman and Sandy Denny.

(•)) The remarkable singer and top exponent of highlife music, Fela Kuti, studied at the Trinity College of Music.

(•)) Engelbert Humperdinck was born into a military family of twelve based in Madras, India. He swapped his engineering job for saxophone playing and eventually singing – during early shows he was supported by an exciting new guitarist called Jimi Hendrix.

(•)) 'Careless Whisper' was written three years before it was released, then released three years before the accompanying solo album.

(•)) Village People mastermind Jacques Morali lost his life to AIDS-related illness in 1991.

(•)) The Seekers' 'The Carnival is Over' sold more copies than The Beatles' 'We Can Work It Out'/'Daytripper'. In doing so, it knocked The Rolling Stones' 'Get Off of My Cloud' from the top spot. That's not right.

((•)) '(We're Gonna) Rock Around the Clock' by Bill Haley And His Comets is considered to be one of, if not *the*, most important catalysts of rock 'n' roll, the music of the younger generation. Yet Haley was thirty years old when it was released, blind in his left eye and overweight – and he co-wrote it with a songwriter who was in his sixties. Decca Records struggled to categorise this new genre of music and so listed the song as 'a foxtrot'.

((•)) Paul Simon's first UK hit was actually by someone else – it came when The Seekers released his song 'Someday, One Day' in 1966.

((•)) Culture Club's 'Karma Chameleon' was a highly unlikely Number 1 single in the traditionally conservative USA.

((•)) Boy George is one of the world's most sought-after DJs.

((•)) A stage invasion for an Oasis *Top of the Pops* appearance was only the second in the TV show's history, the other being for Nirvana's rendition of 'Smells Like Teen Spirit'.

((•)) For their appearance on *Top of the Pops* to promote 'Country House', Blur started the programme by driving into the studio on a milk float.

((•)) Sidney Bechet used to take his saxophone to pieces on stage *while* still playing it.

((•)) Sting was reported to have earned £400,000 in royalties from the sample of 'Every Breath You Take' used by Puff Daddy on his smash hit tribute to Notorious BIG, 'I'll Be Missing You'. The song's popularity endured, coming as it did after the death of Princess Diana.

((•)) Puff Daddy's Bad Boy Entertainment was started in his apartment; he later received $75 million from Arista to allow them to be more involved in the label.

((•)) John Lennon claimed that the opening snarl of feedback on 'I Feel Fine' was the first time this noise had deliberately been recorded for a single release.

((•)) In 1964 The Beatles had no fewer than thirty songs in the US singles charts, peaking one week when they held all top five positions and three of the top four album slots.

((•)) When John Lennon attended a Foyles literary luncheon to mark the success of his rather nonsensical book *In Your Own Write*, his entire speech was, 'Thank you very much, you've got a lucky face.'

((•)) The first Western act to have a single released in China was Wham!.

((•)) Wham!'s 'Last Christmas' remains the biggest selling record never to get to Number 1 (it was kept off the top spot by Band Aid).

((•)) When the Sheffield-based Human League released 'Don't You Want Me?', including the lyric, 'You were working as a waitress in a cocktail bar,' there were no cocktail bars in their home town. This song was Virgin Records' first ever Number 1.

((•)) In terms of registered UK single sales, not one of the one hundred best-selling stars has achieved greater success with any solo single than with a band: not Lennon, not McCartney, not Roger Waters, not George Michael, not Brian May, not any of The Spice Girls and not, er, H from Steps.

((•)) Britney Spears was still only sixteen when she filmed the video for the '...Baby One More Time' single, complete with skimpy 'Catholic schoolgirl' uniforms. The song has been covered by Travis and Barenaked Ladies.

((•)) Country singer-songwriter Roy Acuff once gave a televised lesson in using the yo-yo to US President Richard Nixon.

((•)) Brian May's guitar was made by his father and himself in their garage. One of Big Bill Broonzy's guitars, which he used to court fame as a bluesman of high repute in the 40s and 50s, was made from an old cigar box when he was just eleven – the same material is said to have been used for Charlie Christian's first guitar too.

((•)) John Peel once spent ten hours in Dallas County Jail for committing five traffic violations in the course of a couple of miles.

((•)) John Peel lists his 'greatest talent' as being able to make a sound like a dolphin.

((•)) 'As long as there is breath in my body, John Peel will be on Radio 1.' Former BBC Radio 1 head Matthew Bannister.

((•)) When videos and MTV became pivotal in the success of modern bands by the mid-80s, *NME* ran a front cover feature wondering 'Can Music Survive the Video Virus?'

((•)) When star of *Grease* and *Saturday Night Fever* John Travolta bought a jumbo jet for $60 million, he was told that the problem was there was only one private runway in America that was big enough to accommodate it. So he bought that too.

(◉) In March 1964, The Beatles accounted for 60% of US record sales.

(◉) Famous movie soundtrack writer John Barry (as heard in numerous Bond films, *Superman 2* etc.) worked in his father's cinemas as a boy. Barry was also previously a highly regarded band leader.

(◉) Alfred Hitchcock's classic film *Psycho* was billed thus: 'The Big News Is That *Psycho* is Hitchcock's Greatest Chiller!'; movie buffs place much of the credit for the film's success with the remarkable soundtrack scored by Bernard Herrmann. After all, it is hard to imagine that the film would have had quite the same impact without the horrific screeching of the 'shower scene'.

(◉) Madonna notoriously wanted to be as famous as God. John Lennon caused outrage in 1966 when he said The Beatles would soon be bigger than Jesus. As noted elsewhere in this book, according to some, Eric Clapton is God.

(◉) When Depeche Mode released their single 'Personal Jesus' in 1989, they placed standard classified ads carrying that slogan along with a phone number which, when dialled, played the new song down the line.

(◉) When Soul II Soul were told to either mime or scrap their scheduled appearance on *Top of the Pops* in 1989, they walked.

(◉) Cliff Richard's 100th single was the May 1989 track 'The Best of Me'.

(•)) 'Somebody said to me that The Beatles were anti-materialistic. That's a huge myth. John and I literally used to sit down and say, "Now, let's write a swimming pool."'
Paul McCartney

(•)) It is widely known that Decca declined to sign The Beatles. In fact, they cancelled the audition for which the future Fab Four were booked to play in front of several Decca executives, giving the justification that 'guitar bands are on the way out'. However, they weren't alone: EMI, HMV, Pye and Columbia also turned them down. The Beatles were also turned down by many record companies in the US until Capitol Records saw the light (and the dollar signs).

(•)) Early rock 'n' roll records sold in huge quantities thanks partly to the rise of the newly recognised 'teenager', young kids who were financially buoyant due to strong wages as a result of a labour shortage and eager to enjoy teenage life before the rigours of eighteen months' National Service.

(•)) Dick Clark, presenter of TV show *American Bandstand* in the 50s, earned himself the memorable nickname of 'The World's Oldest Teenager'.

(•)) The phrase 'agitpop' is based on the Russian term *agitprop*, meaning 'propaganda for agitation'.

(•)) According to the BBC, the Children In Need charity single 'Perfect Day', a cover of a Lou Reed track from his 1972 album *Transformer*, included the following musical genres: blues, Britpop, classical, country, easy listening, experimental, gospel, hip-hop, indie, jazz, opera, pop, rap, reggae, rock, soul, trip hop and world music.

(•) The biggest-selling female solo single in UK chart history is not by Madonna, Whitney Houston or Claire from Steps, but Cher ('Believe').

(•) Ross Columbo was an American singer, composer and accomplished violinist active in the first third of the twentieth century. In the early 30s, he played in Bing Crosby's band and went on to enjoy a sex symbol status and a role in the original film version of *Moulin Rouge*. The world, it seemed, was his oyster. However, his death came aged only 26, when a friend touched a match to a loaded gun by mistake and Columbo was killed by the ricocheting bullet.

(•) Bing Crosby is reported to have released 2,600 singles and 125 albums, with an accumulative total record sales figure in excess of 300 million copies. He nicknamed himself 'The Old Groaner'. He was survived by his swing bandleader brother Bob.

(•) Combined record sales for 'Barbie Girl' band Aqua are in excess of 30 million copies. Not laughing now, are you?

(•) Prime Minister Sir Alec Douglas-Home called the Fab Four his 'secret weapon'.

(•) (Little) Stevie Wonder's debut single, 'I Call it Pretty Music (But the Old People Call it the Blues)' was a flop, despite drums played by then session sticksman Marvin Gaye.

(•) Will Young is a non-identical twin. And no, it's not with Gareth Gates.

(((•))) Wet Wet Wet became so concerned about the possible suffocating effects of the colossal sales and over-exposure of their single 'Love is All Around' (taken from the soundtrack to hit movie *Four Weddings and a Funeral*) that their manager was reported to have phoned from abroad to insist on the song being deleted. The song's writer, The Troggs' Reg Presley, declared he would be spending the massive royalties on studying crop circles.

(((•))) 'Disco' was initially a term used to describe dancing to *any* record, rather than to a live band as had previously been the norm.

(((•))) Sly and the Family Stone's 1968 track 'Dance to the Music' is considered by many to be the very first disco song.

(((•))) Donna Summer's 'I Feel Love' is often credited with being the first techno song.

(((•))) At one point in the 80s, there were three different versions of Boney M touring. The man behind the original band was Frankie Farian, also mastermind behind the ultimately ill-fated Milli Vanilli (whose singer committed suicide after it emerged that he and his brother had not sung on their Grammy-winning hits).

(((•))) New York's most famous 'disco', Studio 54, was busted by New York cops posing as drug dealers.

(((•))) Jerome Flynn was booed off stage when his school band System X played Stranglers covers to a crowd of old-age pensioners.

(((•))) Phil Spector withdrew his seasonal song 'A Christmas Gift To You' out of respect for the assassinated US President JF Kennedy.

((•)) In early 1963, weeks before they became the biggest band in the world, The Beatles were still unknown enough to be billed on a Scottish tour as 'The Love Me Do Boys'.

((•)) Frankie Goes To Hollywood struggled to get a record deal at first, perhaps due to their decision to bill themselves as 'post-punk S&M gay cabaret'.

((•)) Very early cabaret was considered far more credible than its latter-day counterpart – Erik Satie often played piano at Parisian cabaret nights. At that point, they did not offer chicken in a basket.

((•)) *Saturday Night Fever* was initially produced as a stop-gap measure to keep John Travolta working while production difficulties on the *Grease* project were resolved.

((•)) Olivia Newton-John is the daughter of Nobel Prize-winning physicist Max Born and she originally harboured ambitions to be a vet.

((•)) Nero did not fiddle while Rome burned. He couldn't play the fiddle. He played the lyre.

((•)) Pope Gregory (pope from AD 590 to 604; later anointed a saint) used to notate music dictated from a dove said to be sent from heaven.

((•)) St Gregory also developed a system of notation using letters of the alphabet (similar to modern staff notation), which was actually the same process used to compose early Lennon and McCartney songs, rather than the more established major and minor scales.

((•)) Elvis Presley, Groucho Marx, Charlie Chaplin and Bing Crosby all died within a few months of each other.

((•)) Wings' 'Mull of Kintyre' was written about the same Mull where a Chinook helicopter crashed in 1994, killing 29 senior military personnel.

((•)) After a live hiatus of five years, in 1972 Paul McCartney – along with his new band Wings – turned up at a student union and played a surprise set in front of five hundred gobsmacked students.

((•)) 'Bohemian Rhapsody' was written by Freddie Mercury after he had spent several weeks researching opera; the recording of the masterpiece took three weeks. When Kenny Everett was asked why he had played the acetate (no less than fourteen times) of the song given to him by his friend Freddie – under strict understanding never to air it on radio – the comedian and DJ said his 'finger slipped'.

((•)) When Pink Floyd played their own 'festival' at Knebworth in 1975, they organised a fly-past by two Spitfire fighter planes.

((•)) The performers on the Live Aid poster were listed alphabetically, rumoured to be a ruse to avoid any rock star ego clashes over who was above whom on the bill. Tickets cost only £25.

((•)) During the recording of Band Aid's 'Do They Know it's Christmas?' at west London studio SARM, the attendant rock stars were instructed to take any complaints directly to Bob Geldof. Nobody did. Music biz legend has it that when the US equivalent, 'We Are the World', was stumbling amid egos and personality clashes, Geldof was flown over, SAS-style, to sort the mess out. It worked.

((•)) Veteran DJ Alan 'Fluff' Freeman got the nickname after wearing an old fluffy jumper to a party.

((•)) Paul McCartney's actual first name is James (Paul is his middle monicker).

((•)) Imelda Marcos once worked as a record shop assistant.

((•)) Elvis Costello once said that 'writing about music is like dancing about architecture'.

((•)) Father of 21, musician Solomon Burke said he read the Bible passage that said 'be fruitful and multiply' but declined to read any farther.

((•)) Stevie Winwood was a Boy Scout.

((•)) In his early days, Bob Seger once played a gig on the same bill as a stripper with a horse as part of her act.

((•)) David Bowie famously agreed with countless bluesmen that rock 'n' roll was the music of the devil. By contrast, Bob Dylan said that politics was 'an instrument of the devil'.

((•)) Scott Weiland, hard-living frontman of pseudo-grungers Stone Temple Pilots, opined that sex, drugs and rock 'n' roll had been replaced by 'crack, masturbation and Madonna'.

((•)) 'Sexual intercourse is a lovely t'ing.'
Bob Marley, 1975

((•)) Dozens of rock stars have served time, usually for drugs offences, drunkenness or public order offences. However, The Clash's Joe

Strummer and Topper Headon were each fined £5 for spraying their band's name on a wall. They were kept in a police cell overnight after failing to appear in court to answer a charge relating to throwing a pillow case from the window of a room at a Holiday Inn.

((•)) The song 'What's the New Mary Jane?' was scheduled for release as the next Beatles single but was never put out due to the band's split.

((•)) Keith Moon prompted The New Yardbirds to change their name after the band overheard the bonkers Who drummer say, 'They went down like a lead zeppelin.'

((•)) At a time when Pete Townshend was recovering from alcohol problems, The Who did a tour sponsored by a brewery.

((•)) At the wedding of the late John Bonham's son, Jason, the surviving members of his father's band Led Zeppelin reunited for the reception. Wouldn't have wanted to be the disco DJ that night.

((•)) When Ian Astbury of The Cult saw a security guard apparently beating up an audience member at his band's Daytona show in 1990, he jumped down into the crowd to placate the situation, only to be beaten up himself.

((•)) Ned's Atomic Dustbin took their name from a sketch in *The Goon Show*.

((•)) Procol Harum was named after a friend's pedigree cat.

((•)) John Lennon and his son Sean were both born on the ninth of the month (October), his mom lived at Number 9 (Newcastle Road), Brian Epstein's first Beatles gig was on 9 November 1961 and Lennon signed a record deal with the rest of the Beatles on 9 May 1962. He met Yoko on 9 November 1966 and when he was killed, his body was taken to the Roosevelt Hospital on 9th Avenue.

(◉) Julian Cope was born in Wales.

(◉) When asked if he had ever had any homosexual experiences, Robyn Hitchcock said, 'Years ago, but that was simply because I was sent to a good school... There weren't any girls around so you had to practise on men.'

(◉) 'The worst crime I can think of would be to pull people off by faking it and pretending as if I'm having a hundred per cent fun. Sometimes I feel as though I should have a punch-in time clock before I walk on stage... it's better to burn out than to fade away.'
Extract from Kurt Cobain's suicide note.

(◉) 'I'm really sorry, you guys. I don't know what I could have done... Just tell [Kurt] he's a fucker, okay? Just say, "Fucker, you're a fucker," and that you love him.' Courtney Love talking to fans after reading out Kurt Cobain's suicide note.

(◉) 'Killing Me Softly with His Song' by Roberta Flack is about Don McLean.

(◉) In the song 'I Want My Baby Back', Jimmy Cross' girlfriend dies in an horrific car crash; the singer can't live without her and three months later digs up her body and joins her in the coffin. Hey, if it worked for Emily Bronte...

(◉) 'The Toy Symphony', often attributed to Haydn, was actually written by Mozart's father, Leopold.

((•)) Emperor Joseph II appears to have suggested the title of *Cosi Fan Tutte*, meaning 'All women behave alike'.

((•)) 'Mark my words, that young fellow is going to cause a stir in the world.' Mozart, on hearing Beethoven improvise at a piano, and thus inventing the A&R man.

((•)) Franz Schubert, towering composer, was actually only just five feet tall. His nickname was Schwammerl, literally meaning 'mushroom', but which translates more accurately as 'fatso'.

((•)) The lyric 'In this ever-changing world in which we live in,' from Paul McCartney's *Live and Let Die* Bond theme tune, the second 'in' is a grammatically incorrect superfluous preposition. Innit.

((•)) The final chord of The Beatles' 'A Day in the Life' lasts 24 seconds.

((•)) Elvis' 'Heartbreak Hotel' was not a UK Number 1 single. Neither was The Who's 'My Generation'.

((•)) When Robert Smith cut off his goth locks in 1986, MTV News broadcast updates every half-hour for a day.

((•)) Pete Townshend is alleged to have done the briefest rock interview of all time, with *Rolling Stone* magazine's Cameron Crowe: 'I've changed my mind.'

((•)) When Decca was handed the initial master tape of the seminal 'My Generation' single, they refused to accept it, complaining that the feedback at the end of the track was unplanned distortion. This was only moderately less embarrassing than EMI, who turned The Who down completely.

(◈) HMV released the first automatically changing record player in 1928, priced exorbitantly at £128.

(◈) Despite The Beatles' global success, in 1969 John Lennon was quoted in the *Daily Express* as saying 'I'm down to my last £50,000.'

(◈) The first UK album chart was published by *Record Retailer* (later to become *Music Week*) in 1960.

(◈) Ever ready with an apt phrase, Pete Townshend himself described The Who (largely pilloried by the establishment in their early days) as purveyors of 'sweet songs sung by a violent group'. Indeed, drummer Keith Moon often had to tie his drum kit together with rope as he hit the skins so hard.

(◈) During the film *Tommy*, Elton John played the Pinball Wizard of the famed song. He stood atop a pair of 54-inch-tall fibreglass Dr Martens boots, his size-four feet fitted into another pair of shoes, which were strapped on top of the towering twelve holers; Elton kept the boots afterwards. In 1988, at a London auction of rock 'n' roll memorabilia, the Chairman of Dr Martens, Stephen Griggs, bought the boots for £12,100. The event was sparked by Elton wanting to 'clear out' some rooms to redecorate – it raised over £4 million.

(◈) In The Who's later film *Quadrophenia*, the central character Jimmy's complex and endearing personality is said to be made up of elements of all four of The Who's personalities – the meaning of the word 'quadrophenia'.

((•)) The year punk broke – 1976 – was also the driest summer since 1727.

((•)) When The Sex Pistols played an early gig in Manchester, the crowd was small but enthusiastic, and contained amongst others Ian Curtis, Bernard Sumner and Peter Hook (all later of Joy Division), Tony Wilson (who would later form Factory Records) and Steven Patrick Morrissey.

((•)) Although known for releasing the first ever punk single ('New Rose' in 1976), The Damned were also the first British punk band to hit the USA, in April 1977. When they returned to their hotel room afterwards, they found several gifts left for them by The Rolling Stones, including a birthday cake and seven meringue pies.

((•)) The Clash's eponymously titled debut album was recorded in just three weekends.

((•)) At an early gig by The Specials, mainman Jerry Dammers' keyboard proved too heavy to raise on to the stage; he played from the floor among the crowd instead. Incidentally, Dammers was the son of a clergyman.

((•)) The first ever 'Two Tone' track was the eponymous single recorded by The Selecter – in the garden shed of producer Roger Lomas.

((•)) In late 50s Jamaica, bassist Cluet Johnson played his brand of new music around town while greeting people with the phrase 'Love Skavoovie', from which the word 'ska' is said by some to have been derived. Others claim it is derived from the sound of the hi-hat being opened and closed.

(•) Heavyweight 350-pounder Buster Bloodvessel of Bad Manners has a thirteen-inch tongue, is totally bald and holds the world record for eating Big Macs – thirty in a row. He can also fit an entire Big Mac in his mouth.

(•) In his last ever interview before his assassination, John Lennon said he admired Madness.

(•) In May 1964, Radio Caroline started broadcasting off the UK coast; however, it wasn't alone. Its less famous seaborne rival was Radio Atlanta.

(•) After having served so much of their hard-working apprentice-ship in Germany, it was not perhaps all that surprising that The Beatles issued German-language versions of some of their hits, including 'Komm, Gib Mir Deine Hand' ('I Want to Hold Your Hand'). Not quite the same, is it?

(•) The one-off single 'Pamela Jean' was released by The Survivors – a pseudonym for The Beach Boys.

(•) More than a dozen Beach Boys songs have studio talking and chit-chat in the background.

(•) The Beach Boys' 'Surfin'' was actually composed on a beach. Between 1974 and 1976, Brian Wilson never set foot outside his house.

(•) There are still numerous theories and urban myths about a 'lost masterpiece' that Beach Boys maestro Brian Wilson is said to have destroyed in a fit of paranoia.

((•)) The Beach Boys' album *Pet Sounds*, which tops many magazine polls as the greatest album of all time, did not sell well on its initial release.

((•)) At one point, Brian Wilson's mental problems reportedly led him to play a piano stuck in a sand box. He said this was to help him get in touch with his 'inner child'.

((•)) Phil Spector sings backing vocals on the John Lennon track 'Oh Yoko'.

((•)) When Bruce Springsteen was at his 80s peak, he turned down $10 million to advertise for car manufacturer Chrysler.

((•)) Fifteen artists in the US Rock And Roll Hall Of Fame have also sung adverts for Coca-Cola.

((•)) The famous loved-up Woodstock festival of August 1969 was intended to be a highly organised and commercially minded event. Originally, there were 186,000 tickets sold, with police expecting around two hundred thousand people to attend at most. However, on the weekend in question, over one million turned up at Max Yasgur's farm in Bethel, New York. Within hours, the $18 entrance fee was abandoned and the event turned into a free festival, as security could do little to keep the swarming masses out. As the most chronicled example of its genre, these 'Three Days of Peace and Music' saw three deaths, two births and four miscarriages.

((•)) Nirvana's debut album *Bleach* was produced for just $606.17.

(•) Noel Gallagher of Oasis suffered from a kidney infection as a child and was allowed to wear long trousers to school to keep him warm as he would have been susceptible to infection.

(•) During the Second World War, US paratroopers were the first Westerners to cut their hair in a Mohican style as a gesture of solidarity in the face of the forthcoming jump across the Rhine. In England in the 50s, Mancunian hairdresser George Mason offered a reward of £1 to the first youth who turned up at his salon and requested a 'mohican'. The winner, fifteen-year-old errand boy John Ross, was asked only to recommend the salon to his friends. He can comfortably claim to have predated such legendary godfathers of punk as Iggy Pop and Joe Strummer by at least twenty years.

(•) Dr Martens boots, which have been tied inextricably to youth culture since their inception in 1960, were almost called Dr Funck (the other partner in the duo who invented the famous air-cushioned sole) but the company opted for the former because Funck sounded too much like 'fuck'.

(•) Thigh-high boots were originally worn by pirates and smugglers because they could easily hide stolen and smuggled valuables in them – hence they were called 'bootleggers', a term still used today.

(•) Like their Western counterparts decades beforehand, worried Chinese authorities for a long time tried to suppress the rise of rock music. A ban was imposed and a pamphlet issued entitled 'How to Recognise Pornographic Music', which even listed jazz among the forbidden styles.

(•) Gwen Stefani's brother dropped out of his sister's band No Doubt to become a cartoonist for *The Simpsons*.

(◉) Perhaps music isn't the universal language after all – it took radio over forty years to get a global audience of 50 million; it took television fifteen years to do the same. The Internet achieved that in less than 36 months.

(◉) Cassette recorders were introduced in 1963.

(◉) At one point in 1988, some newspapers were claiming that U2 frontman Bono had been added to the IRA's hit list.

(◉) Madonna made her Broadway debut in *Speed the Plow* in March 1988.

(◉) During the peak of the 'home taping kills music' crisis in the late 80s, the Government considered putting a hefty levy on blank cassettes.

(◉) Skinheads were previously known as 'hard mods'. Early skinhead culture adored soul and Jamaican ska. Parties in Brixton and Lambeth played such music and thus introduced Rude Boy culture into England.

(◉) One band on The Beatles' Apple label was called Elephant's Memory.

(◉) Previous to becoming Led Zeppelin's manager, Peter Grant was a bouncer and a movie extra. He weighed more than 300 lb.

(◉) Bruce Springsteen once said the two most unpopular things in his childhood home were him and his guitar.

(◉)) Images of Elvis, Bill Haley, Buddy Holly, Clyde McPhatter, Otis Redding, Dinah Washington and Hank Williams have all appeared on US postage stamps.

(◉)) Skiffle is a widely known genre of music but it was also what West Indian skinheads sometimes called their cropped haircuts, frequently embellished with a pencil-thin shaved parting.

(◉)) The 1969 song 'Skinhead Moonstomp' by Symarip was a hit with underground skin circles – Symarip was a pseudonym for The Pyramids.

(◉)) Originally, executives wanted The Who to star in their classic film *Quadrophenia*, but the band were anxious to avoid reducing the movie's appeal in the US and so helped choose a relatively unknown cast, including Sting (playing a character called 'Ace Face').

(◉)) Ironically, given The Who's later championing by Vespa-riding mods, their own mod incarnation as The High Numbers with the single 'I'm the Face' was a flop.

(◉)) Phil Daniels, who starred as 'Jimmy the Mod' in *Quadrophenia*, later became a Royal Shakespearean actor in the RSC's performance of *A Clockwork Orange*; he also formed his own band called Phil Daniels and the Cross and made cameo appearances in Blur's 'Parklife' song and the acceompanying video.

(◉)) The jester in Shakespeare's *Twelfth Night*, Feste, would entertain and comment on the play's plots by means of song.

(◉)) Bessie Smith is widely crowned as 'The Empress of the Blues'. Her massive success earned huge sums, but her duplicitous husband siphoned off funds to finance the showbiz career of his mistress. The Empress died in a car crash and was buried in an unmarked grave until Janis Joplin – a big fan – and some friends paid for a headstone in 1970.

((•)) In the first week of its 1987 release, Michael Jackson's *Bad* sold almost as many copies as the rest of the UK Top 30 put together.

((•)) In 1987 *Top of the Pops* was launched in the US but was a complete flop.

((•)) After the tabloid hysteria and exaggeration about The Beastie Boys' alleged anti-social behaviour – including one story they vigorously denied claiming they had told a group of disabled fans to 'Go away you f***ing cripples!' – the Beastie Boys each received death threats.

((•)) The Cure were none too pleased when they found out some right-wing DJs in America were using their single 'Killing an Arab' to incite racial hatred.

((•)) In 1986 an 'anti-smack' drug awareness charity single was released that included Sir Cliff, Nik Kershaw and Howard Jones.

((•)) Gary Glitter supported Wham! at their final concert at Wembley Stadium in the summer of 1986.

((•)) Sigue Sigue Sputnik offered to sell advertising space in the gaps between the tracks on their debut album.

((•)) Glam rock was known as 'glitter rock' in the US, where it made very little impact – apart from Ziggy of course, if you can call him glam. Perhaps the sole US glam band of note was Zolar-X, big fans of Kubrick's *A Clockwork Orange*.

(•))) Mini-Moog synthesisers were first introduced in 1970, with enthusiastic commentators predicting the end of guitar music. One year later, Led Zeppelin released *Led Zeppelin IV*, featuring their masterpiece of protracted rock, 'Stairway to Heaven'.

(•))) Fleetwood Mac was one of the very first bands to use digital technology in 1979. *NME* reported the news and noted that the technology, although virtually unheard of, was 'hailed as the biggest advance since stereo-digital recording'. The production suite to use these rudimentary digital facilities cost at least $100,000, but nonetheless the members of the Mac were way ahead of their time.

(•))) Little Feat's mainman Lowell George died of complications related to a big problem: obesity.

(•))) In 1979, some of Iggy Pop's UK tour dates were cancelled, not because the venues disliked the Ig but because former Sex Pistol Glen Matlock was in his backing band.

(•))) When The Sex Pistols released 'God Save the Queen' in the Jubilee year of 1977, many record stores refused to stock it and one radio station even pretended that it didn't exist.

(•))) Alice Cooper's on-stage pal, a lengthy boa constrictor snake, died when it was bitten by a rat that was supposed to have become its dinner.

(•))) Linda Ronstadt was once offered $1 million to pose nude for *Hustler*. She declined.

((•)) The Sex Pistols' first record contract with EMI lasted three months; their second, with A&M, lasted a week.

((•)) Patti Smith once broke her neck after falling off stage.

((•)) Texan Roky Erickson was in The 13th Floor Elevators, and thus very much part of the 60s LSD-fuelled culture. When he was found with a joint and arrested, his lawyer suggested he plead insanity. He was promptly placed in Rusk State Hospital for the Criminally Insane *for three years*, during which time he was given electro-shock therapy and powerful medication. On his release he was a pale imitation of his former self. By 1982 he signed an affidavit that he was 'inhabited by an alien' and spent much of the 90s on social security benefits before another spell in an asylum.

((•)) Many experts argue that the classic sci-fi film *2001: A Space Odyssey* features cinematic history's finest soundtrack.

((•)) Stanley Kubrick counted 241 walk-outs from the cinema by film executives when *2001: A Space Odyssey* was previewed. One executive was overheard saying, 'Well, that's the end of Stanley Kubrick.' It won him his only Oscar.

((•)) Perhaps no other film has become a greater influence on musical culture than Stanley Kubrick's highly controversial Oscar-nominated *A Clockwork Orange*. Based on the Anthony Burgess book of the same name, the film centres around the scientific 'rehabilitation' of Alex Delarge (played by Malcolm McDowell), who undergoes a 'cure for criminals.' The unique vocabulary featured in the film – the gang members were called 'droogs', their language itself named 'nadsat', seemingly half-Cockney, half-Russian – added to its allure, as did the affront caused by the 'ultra-violence', namely graphic acts of barbarity, including sexual assaults. A huge crossover with musical subcultures has occurred in the film's wake, with several bands drawing directly on it for inspiration. Major Accident, The Violators, Blitz, King and The Clockwork Soldiers all openly admired Kubrick's work, while California's Durango 95 took their name from the car driven by the droogs in the film. The Adicts were perhaps the biggest fans, with lead singer Monkey dressing up head-to-toe as a Clockwork skin and aping Alex Delarge's disconcerting grin to perfection. The band's album artwork also depicted scenes from the film.

((•)) The Heaven Seventeen was the name of one of the acts on the cardboard album separators in the record shop in the film *A Clockwork Orange* – or it may have been the chart listing in the shop – and is where Heaven 17 got their name from. The band Moloko also took their name from the film – 'moloko' was a drug-infused milk.

((•)) *Rolling Stone* magazine was launched in 1967.

((•)) Roy Orbison wrote his biggest hit, 'Only the Lonely', intending it to be sung by The Everly Brothers.

((•)) In the early 70s, The Bee Gees were pencilled in to make a horror movie called *Castle X*, set and filmed in Yugoslavia. Fortunately for all concerned, it was shelved.

((•)) After learning that a ceasefire had been declared in most of Vietnam in 1973, Neil Young stopped mid-concert and announced, 'Peace has come.'

((•)) German band Saturnalia released the world's first 3D picture disc in February 1973.

(◉) Although it never hit the top spot in the US album charts, Pink Floyd's *Dark Side of the Moon* stayed in the US album lists for 625 weeks, finally dropping off thirteen years after its release.

(◉) When The Sex Pistols played a gig at St Martin's School of Art in November 1975, the manager was so irate at the noise they were making he simply pulled the plug out of the PA after only five songs.

(◉) 'Barry White's three best qualities are his love for music, his love for people and his love for himself.'
Barry White

(◉) 'If it was 1965 and we'd just put out our second album, we'd absolutely be the pop kings of the world. It would've been The Beatles, The Rolling Stones, Oasis and then The Who. I firmly believe that.'
Noel Gallagher, 1997

(◉) Reminiscing about his first meeting with Jimi Hendrix, Eric Clapton said the latter spent 'a lot of his time combing his hair'.

(◉) 'Rock 'n' roll is supposed to be fun. You remember fun, don'tcha?'
Johnny Rotten, 1978

(◉) In 1990, an American promoter offered £30,000 to The Sex Pistols to re-form – on condition that it was *without* Johnny Rotten.

(◉) In 1989, with the CD only just around the corner, vinyl sales plunged but strangely cassette sales went up 500%.

(◉) A UK MP called for a ban on a Guns N' Roses T-shirt that showed a woman apparently being sexually assaulted by a robot.

(◉) Pink Floyd's inflatable pig was once the centre of a legal row between Roger Waters and his estranged ex-bandmates.

(◉) Bros' last ever gig was at Wembley Stadium; not long before, a record store signing at HMV Oxford Street had seen central London gridlocked as 11,000 screaming fans turned up.

(◉) The Grand Ole Opry started broadcasting from Nashville's radio station WSM in December 1927. It was initially aimed at the local agricultural population.

(◉) Globally, Bing Crosby notched up over three hundred hits.

(◉) When he was asked what the most intelligent thing he had ever heard anyone say in rock 'n' roll, Paul Simon replied, 'Be-bop-a-lula, she's my baby.'

(◉) Buzzcocks took their name from a headline in London's weekly magazine *Time Out*.

(◉) 'I hope I'll not be seeing you again.' Bill Grundy to The Sex Pistols after they swore on his TV show in December 1976, causing national outrage and infamous tabloid headlines such as 'The Filth and the Fury'.

(◉) Legendary record sleeve designer Malcolm Garrett painted his pair of Dr Martens boots bright orange to coincide with the release of the similarly coloured Buzzcocks' debut album, *Another Music in a Different Kitchen*.

(•)) The Bee Gees made a disastrous film version of *Sergeant Pepper's Lonely Hearts Club Band*.

(•)) The fleeting post-punk genre of Oi! is said to have got its name either from the Cockney pronunciation of 'hey' or the Greek phrase for 'common people', namely 'hoi polloi'. Given that Oi! fans wore knee-high DMs, had names like Cock Sparrer and Slaughter and the Dogs and played gigs that were prone to erupt in violence, my money's not on the Greek option.

(•)) Calypso is a word associated with music and musical culture – yet Calypso is the Greek goddess of silence.

(•)) Sham 69 take their name from an abbreviation of 'Hersham'.

(•)) At many gigs by Peter and the Test Tube Babies, security and police insisted fans took out their shoe and boot laces to minimize the chances of fighting in the audience during the set.

(•)) The large leather cherry-red boots worn by so-called 'scooter boys' were a deliberate ploy to separate this clique from the black-and-white bowling shoes worn by fans of The Jam.

(•)) The then revolutionary portable Sony Walkman was launched the same year as Trivial Pursuit. Standard Walkmans carry one album; the most advanced Apple iPods can carry ten thousand songs... and are smaller.

(•)) When Run DMC appeared in their videos (most notably for 'Walk This Way' with Aerosmith) wearing the classic Adidas Super Star trainer – minus the laces – that shoe company saw sales explode exponentially within hours. In 1986, the same band recorded a track called 'My Adidas'.

(◈) When Madness and The Specials toured together in 1979, the tour bus stopped at a fish and chip shop, whereupon Specials leader Jerry Dammers walked in and ordered 27 cod and chips, five plaice, three gherkins, an Irn Bru and a Kit-Kat.

(◈) Ska legend Clement 'Sir Coxsone' Dodd took his full name after the Yorkshire cricketer.

(◈) For a while, Bob Marley wore a crew cut.

(◈) Richard the Lionheart was also a *trouvere*, the musical companion of the troubadour.

(◈) A serenade is the playing of music to 'a fair lady in the evening'; if she likes a lie-in and you find yourself still playing in the morning, your romantic musical mission then becomes known as an *aubade*, from the French word for 'dawn'.

(◈) Michael Jackson might consider himself the King of Pop, but he is most definitely not its patron saint. That accolade goes to St Cecilia of the second century AD, who became the first pop idol by singing hymns as she was scalded to death in a vat of boiling water.

(◈) When the compact disc was introduced in 1983, vinyl manufacturers were generally sceptical it would catch on. A few clever ones secretly bought CD manufacturing machinery.

(•)) The spiral whirls on a CD that contain the data are two and a half miles long – which perhaps explains why listening to a Westlife album leads to such a mind-numbing headache.

(•)) The first million-selling CD was Dire Straits' *Brothers in Arms*. It sold fifteen million copies worldwide. Hard to believe, I know.

(•)) Lionel Bart's place in musical history is secured by having written *Oliver!*. But before that he was in a skiffle group called The Cavemen alongside Tommy Steele. He is also the writer behind Cliff Richard's 'Living Doll'.

(•)) Musicians in New Orleans' red-light area would play in brothels and bars to entertain the clientele, particularly those found along Basin Street. Over the years, a distinctive free-flowing and improvisational style emerged from those seedy establishments that eventually coalesced enough to be given a name: jazz.

(•)) On its initial dissemination out of New Orleans whorehouses and bars into the wider public market place, jazz was seen as a genuine threat to good Christian social order.

(•)) Dizzy Gillespie's autobiography carried the excellent title *To Bop or Not to Bop*.

(•)) The word 'jazz' may have come from the French for 'cat', namely *jaser*. Others suggest its first incarnation was possibly 'jass', which, in New Orleans street slang, meant sexual intercourse. One theory has it that, as Johnny Stein was leading out his band in 1916 (in Chicago, oddly enough), an unknown audience member shouted out, 'Jass it up, boys!'

(⟨⟨⟩⟩) So-called 'rags and stomps' were composed by largely illiterate and desperately poor black immigrants in the southern United States. Reeling from appalling treatment by slave masters and a deeply bigoted society, these coerced and oppressed groups used anything to make music and thus lighten their life, even washboards. From the crude but liberating crevices of ragtime came the first shoots of jazz.

(⟨⟨⟩⟩) According to musicologist Alan Blackwood, the simplest definition of the blues is 'a sung lament'.

(⟨⟨⟩⟩) Many early blues songs spoke of oppression, drink, violence, hard labour and all manner of awful elements of the suppressed black southern population's life, even including the dreaded crop-destroyer, the boll weevil.

(⟨⟨⟩⟩) Bluesman Huddie Ledbetter, better known as Leadbelly, served time in a chain gang.

(⟨⟨⟩⟩) Many blues pianists prefer a so-called 'honky tonk' instrument that is slightly out of tune, as a rigidly tuned standard piano would sterilise the emotional nuances of the music (much of which revolves around the flattening or diminishing of the third and seventh notes of the major scale). These are referred to as the 'blue notes'.

(⟨⟨⟩⟩) The phrase 'Tin Pan Alley' was coined by a musician walking along West 28th Street in Manhattan and hearing the din coming out of the windows where hard-up songwriters were hard at work. (London's Denmark Street was, to a lesser extent, the UK equivalent.) The man most associated with Tin Pan Alley, music publisher Harry Von Tilzer, had previously been a circus performer.

((•)) One of Tin Pan Alley's most prolific writing houses was the so-called Brill Building. Once writers were recruited to the firm, they were given a cubicle each, which simply contained a desk, some pencils, some paper and a piano. This brutally direct approach to songwriting brought us Neil Diamond, Carole King and Neil Sedaka.

((•)) Phil Spector, super-producer who called his technique the 'Wall of Sound', was once an assistant to Leiber and Stoller and also wrote with Gene Pitney.

((•)) The jazz song 'St Louis Blues', by luminary WC Handy, has been recorded more than any other track from that genre.

((•)) The term 'Blues' derives from the sixteenth century term 'blue devils'.

((•)) Neil Diamond wrote The Monkees' biggest hit, 'I'm a Believer'.

((•)) Madness were originally called The Aldenham Glamour Boys, then The North London Invaders. Chrissie Boy Foreman and Lee Thompson of that band met while they were both working as gardeners. Singer Suggs was once thrown out of the band for missing rehearsals and going to see Chelsea FC instead.

((•)) Sting was a regular on the live jazz club scene before forming The Police.

((•)) Jonathan King produced early Bay City Rollers material.

((•)) On the sleeve of their classic album *One Step Beyond*, Madness stickered the words 'Pay no more than £3.99', making them one of the first bands to use such pocket-friendly tactics.

(◉) American 'Straight Edge' bands (such as Minor Threat, led by the enigmatic Ian McKaye) were so-called because of their rejection of traditional rock 'n' roll excesses such as drugs and drink.

(◉) When Henry Rollins' band Black Flag delivered their first album to their record label, they were told it could not possibly be released due to its 'outrageous content'. Rather than tone the record down, Black Flag released it themselves.

(◉) *Alternative Press* magazine hailed Nico's 1969 album *The Marble Index* as the first ever 'goth' record.

(◉) The famous goth hang-out – or should that be haunt? – the Batcave occupied the very same venue as one of the New Romantics' essentials clubs, Gossips.

(◉) In 1973, Traffic's percussionist Rebop was fined £20 for biting a cab driver's ear.

(◉) Keith Emerson suffered serious hand injuries when a piano that had been rigged with theatrical explosives detonated prematurely at a gig in San Francisco, in February 1974.

(◉) Mary Woodson, girlfriend of Al Green, was so distraught when she spilled boiling grits over him by accident that she promptly shot herself to death at his home. He later announced that more of his stage show would be dedicated to God in her memory.

(◉) The mecca for psychobillly bands in the early 80s was the so-called Klubfoot at the Clarendon in Hammersmith, west London; the record attendance there is held by the Guana Batz.

(◦) King Kurt fans were often dragged out of the crowd, tied to a spinning wheel, given vast quantities of snakebite through a funnel and hose and plastered with bagfuls of flour, all the time being spun on the 'wheel of misfortune' until the inevitable spray of vomit ended the game with a huge cheer from the audience.

(◦) The simple hybrid of 'hillbilly' and 'rock 'n' roll', rockabilly's first generation enjoyed a brief spell of popularity lasting only around three years. 'Blue Suede Shoes' by Carl Perkins was the epitome of the genre, neatly encapsulating the awful poverty that might lead a man to be so protective of his cherished footwear.

(◦) One early rockabilly performer was Roy Orbison – minus the trademark dark glasses – in his band Roy Orbison and the Teen Kings.

(◦) Nick Rhodes, keyboard player with 80s pop band Duran Duran, insisted that the after-show party following his band's 2004 five-night sell-out of Wembley Arena was held at the Grill Room in the Café Royal, Regent Street, London. The reason for this was that Rhodes had learnt that following the final show of Ziggy Stardust's career, after which Bowie killed the character off, David had also held his after-show party at this venue.

(◦) Paul King, the former VH-1 VJ, was frontman for UK pop band King. They were famed for their multi-coloured Dr Martens boots and mullet hair – they called themselves 'psychedelic skins' and 'multi-tone'. King's manager Perry Haines went on to found and edit seminal fashion magazine *i-D*.

(◦) 'Jangly guitars do not my plonker pull.'
Billy Duffy of The Cult

(((•))) Anti-racist skinhead band The Redskins were originally called No Swastikas, and lead singer Chris Dean, aka X. Moore, was a writer for *NME*. They were one of many such anti-racist bands, often clustered together under the banner SHARP (Skinheads Against Racial Prejudice).

(((•))) Just over eighteen months after the 'Nelson Mandela Concert' at Wembley stadium, the imprisoned anti-apartheid campaigner was free. Four years later, in 1994, he was President of South Africa.

(((•))) *Newsweek* once said that grunge was what happened when kids from divorced families got their hands on guitars.

(((•))) By 1994, country music was US radio's most popular musical format.

(((•))) The industrial scene has given us some of the finest band names of all-time: Skinny Puppy; My Life With The Thrill Kill Kult; Revolting Cocks; Sheep On Drugs; Foreheads In A Fishtank; Einstürzende Neubaten; and Throbbing Gristle.

(((•))) Einstürzende Neubaten's lead singer Blixa Bargeld was said to be so passionate about the creation of new sounds and samples that he once wired up his chest to a microphone and four-track, pressed 'record' then got a friend to break his rib, thus capturing the sound on tape.

(((•))) Suede were once hailed on the front cover of the now defunct *Melody Maker* as 'The best new band in Britain' (mind you, so were Menswear and Gay Dad). At the time, Suede had not released a single song.

((•)) It was said that Blur's Anglocentric pivotal second album, *Modern Life is Rubbish*, which is seen by many as opening the floodgates of Britpop, was provisionally titled *We Hate America*.

((•)) Gwen Stefani of No Doubt fame has her own fashion label called L.A.M.B.

((•)) The death of Britpop is seen by most commentators to have been the night the Oasis vs Blur chart race for Number 1 made it on to *The Six O'Clock News*.

((•)) The Levellers took their name from seventeenth-century disenfranchised groups fighting for land and civil rights.

((•)) At the 1975 Windsor Free Festival, prior to which the tabloids had whipped public opinion and establishment anxiety into a feverish pitch about the 'anti-social' travelling community, seven picnickers, five onlookers, nine journalists and four welfare organisations were watched over by 350 riot police.

((•)) Brian May played a guitar solo perched on top of Buckingham Palace to celebrate the Queen's Golden Jubilee. That should be in the dictionary as the definition of 'bizarre'.

((•)) Nu-metal was initially called rapcore.

((•)) In 2000, a massive research project announced that the most performed song of the twentieth century was 'Happy Birthday'.

((•)) By 2002, MTV was being beamed into 250 million homes worldwide.

(•)) The Strokes' singer, Julian Casablancas, is the son of John Casablancas, founder of the all-conquering model agency Elite, who is famed for his scathing views on some elements of the modelling world: he refused to continue working with Naomi Campbell and called Heidi Klum 'a German sausage'.

(•)) Julian Casablancas went to an ultra-exclusive 'finishing school' in Switzerland. L'Institut Le Rosey was one of the world's oldest private schools, costing in the region of £10,000 a term. Although Le Rosey has vehemently denied rumours that Osama bin Laden was once a pupil there, it is a fact that Ben Gautrey of The Cooper Temple Clause attended when he was just six, as did another future Strokes member, Albert Hammond Jr.

(•)) Even before The Velvet Underground (who took their name from the cover of a book about S&M), Lou Reed was a music veteran, having spent time as a contracted songwriter for Pickwick Records. When he finally left the band in 1970, his parents picked him up for the drive to Long Island, where he initially worked as a typist for $40 a week.

(•)) Janis Joplin said one of the hardest elements of playing live was 'making love to 25,000 people on stage then going home alone'.

(•)) It is said that maestro guitarist Stevie Ray Vaughan's fingers were once so blistered and sore that it made it impossible to continue playing for a crucial recording session; the story goes that, by way of remedy, he super-glued his fingertips on to his forearm before ripping the skin off. The theory was that the extra layer of skin would provide a comforting buffer between the sores and the strings. Albert Hammond Jr of The Strokes is also said to have resorted to this rather painful fix.

((•)) Albert Hammond Sr, father of his namesake in The Strokes, was raised in Gibraltar and enjoyed a career as a noted songwriter in the 70s, particularly with the pop hits 'It Never Rains in Southern California' and 'Down by the River'. He has since written tunes for Celine Dion, Julio Iglesias and Chicago.

((•)) The White Stripes' singer Jack White (née Gillis) used to run his own upholstery business in Detroit. He would often write poems and letters addressed to future upholsterers and hide them within the belly of furniture he was recovering – thus ensuring that the only people who would ever see such missives were fellow upholsterers.

((•)) Jack White and Meg White of The White Stripes were initially rumoured to be girlfriend and boyfriend, then brother and sister, then husband and wife; in fact, it later transpired they were divorced.

((•)) Jack White collects stuffed animals and clocks.

((•)) Detroit, the so-called Motor City and home to Motown and garage rock, saw the very first four-cylinder, single block gasoline engine way back in 1896. This momentous event formed the very foundation of that city's love affair with the motor vehicle.

((•)) Motown is an abbreviation of 'Motortown', one of Detroit's nicknames, alongside 'Motor City'.

((•)) Reggae was originally known in 40s Jamaica as 'mento'.

((•)) Funk evolved in New Orleans when pianists created left-hand grooves called 'funky' and bassists wrote often highly complex lines to complement this new style.

((•)) *Discotheque* is actually the combination of the French words for disc and library.

((•)) Disco music rarely dips below 70 beats per minute, the normal pulse rate of humans.

((•)) The term 'heavy metal' was first used by novelist William Burroughs in his book *The Naked Lunch*, then later by Steppenwolf in their hit song 'Born to be Wild'.

((•)) The Rolling Stones were once called 'anti-parent symbols' by the *Daily Mirror*.

((•)) The Rolling Stones' first Top Twenty hit, 'I Wanna be Your Man', was written by Lennon and McCartney.

((•)) Beatles manager Brian Epstein was originally in charge of a local record shop, looking after his father's NEMS shop, just around the corner from The Beatles' mecca of The Cavern Club. After he got several requests for an imported German record by a band called Tony Sheridan with the Beat Brothers (the latter being the Fab Four), a historical union began to unfold.

((•)) Skiffle music used very basic instruments, including washboards, thimbles and tea-chest basses. The most famous skiffle musician is Lonnie Donegan, whose 1956 hit 'Rock Island Line' was arguably the genre's highest-profile success.

((•)) Elvis was a truck driver before he was The King.

((•)) Phil Collins had a small part in The Beatles' film *A Hard Day's Night*.

(•)) Although Sid Vicious died from a heroin overdose, the amount he ingested was not unusual for a frequent user. The problem was that while in prison on charges of murdering his girlfriend Nancy Spungen, Vicious had had to undergo a detoxification course. Thus, when he was released from jail pending a hearing, his body's tolerance of the hard drug was notably reduced.

(•)) The Clash's first US tour was in February 1979.

(•)) When reggae legend Pete Tosh was kept in overnight on marijuana charges by Jamaican police in late 1978, he emerged the next day with a broken arm and head wounds that required twenty stitches.

(•)) In September 1978, Teddy Pendergrass played a gig 'for women only'.

(•)) Columbia Records released its first output in 1891 as cylinder recordings.

(•)) When Bryan Adams' first album flopped, he threatened to release a follow-up entitled *Bryan Adams Hasn't Heard of You Either*.

(•)) Iggy Pop and his Stooges are universally cited as one of Detroit's finest rock 'n' roll bands – in fact they don't come from Detroit, but from the neighbouring town of Ann Arbor.

(•)) Blues legend Son House served a year in jail for manslaughter in 1928, having killed someone in self-defence. Within a year of being set free, he was spotted by Paramount Records and became one of the early twentieth century's most influential bluesmen. Yet he 'retired' from music in 1948 aged only 46, went underground and wasn't seen for twenty years. Then he was 'discovered', infirm, alcoholic and almost incapable of playing the instrument that he was once a complete master of, but he recovered to record several albums before his death in 1988.

(•)) Bluesman Lightnin' Hopkins was able to recite new songs almost off the top of his head and with remarkable fertility. When he died, he had released over one hundred original albums.

(•)) 'Cowboy songs' were popular in vaudeville and music hall. Many of the original generation of cowboy song performers were bona fide 'singing cowboys', such as Jules Verne Allen, before the likes of Roy Rogers turned the genre into just another art form.

(•)) Iggy Pop is regarded as one of the first exponents of the crowd surf. When he first started the practice, however, many audiences would simply part like the Red Sea and watch in bemusement as he crashed to the floor.

(•)) Iggy Pop quit the Stooges after a disastrous gig at the Michigan Palace when a Detroit biker gang fought with the band.

(•)) The Gold Dollar, central venue for the most recent genesis of Detroit garage bands such as The Von Bondies and The White Stripes, was formerly a drag show bar. Jack White carved the sign on the front of the venue.

(•)) Toe Rag Studios in east London, owned by Liam Watson, is supposedly famous for not having a single piece of equipment that dates from after 1963; in fact, this is nonsense, much of the studio gear actually being original or modified equipment from the 80s.

((•)) The Macombo blues club on the south side of Chicago, home to performers such as Lionel Hampton, Louis Jordan, Ella Fitzgerald and Louis Armstrong, was owned by two Polish immigrants, the brothers Leonard and Phil Chess – the very same Chess family name behind the famous record label (although it was initially called Aristocrat).

((•)) Country legend Patsy Cline started off as a tap dancer, learning the skill from the age of four; she died in the same plane crash that killed Hawkshaw Hawkins and Cowboy Copas.

((•)) The Jam were managed by Paul Weller's father, a former feather-weight boxer-turned-taxi driver and builder. One of the band's early break-throughs came when they won an audition on *Opportunity Knocks*.

((•)) Jools Holland's passport states his profession as 'musician'.

((•)) Dyslexic Shaun Ryder is said to have told his school careers officer he wanted to be a journalist and then a porn star in Germany.

((•)) Although the members of New Order were founding partners in the Hacienda nightclub along with Tony Wilson, supremo of Factory Records, drummer Stephen Morris states that he still had to pay to get in on the first night. The club is said to have cost its owners £400,000 in the first two years alone, although by that point *Time* magazine had declared it to be 'the world's most famous nightclub'.

((•)) Glam rock was once described as music played by 'hod carriers in Bacofoil'.

((•)) The Fall are named after a novel by Albert Camus. In 1999, Fall mainstay Mark E. Smith expressed admiration for Pete Waterman, Karlheinz Stockhausen and German Chancellor Bismarck, all in the same interview.

(((•))) Jacqueline Du Pré was given a priceless seventeeth-century Stradivarius cello by an anonymous benefactor when she was only sixteen. Just as well she was good.

(((•))) Natalie Cole sang 'with' her late father on the 1991 version of his classic 'Unforgettable' via the genius of studio wizardry, which allowed them both to appear as if singing a live duet.

(((•))) Ray Charles had one of the finest album titles of all time with his *Genius + Soul = Jazz* ('Genius' being one of his nicknames).

(((•))) In his solo effort based on the 50s sci-fi epic *The Day the Earth Stood Still*, ex-Beatle Ringo Starr was featured in artwork dressed in a spaceman's outfit announcing, 'Klaatu Barada Nikto'.

(((•))) *Sergeant Pepper* took seven hundred hours to record.

(((•))) Ecstasy, the drug of choice for the rave generation, was once called 'penicillin for the soul'.

(((•))) Joy Division's early EP 'An Ideal for Living' was funded by a small bank loan of £400. The late Ian Curtis, who killed himself in 1980, suffered a severe epileptic fit after their very first gig at the Hope and Anchor in Islington, north London. His epilepsy plagued him until his death.

(((•))) The BBC banned The Who's 'My Generation' for a while in 1965, arguing that Roger Daltrey's famous stumbling vocals were 'detrimental to stutterers'; later, during the first Gulf War, the BBC also banned John Lennon's 'Give Peace a Chance' and, for some God-only-knows-why reason, Lulu's Eurovision entry, 'Boom Bang-a-Bang'.

(•) 'Crazy Diamond' Syd Barrett was alleged to have taken LSD almost daily for three solid years. During that spell of narcotic excess, he went on tour with Pink Floyd and often took to the stage with a mixture of drugs and Brylcreem in his permed hair. His later disappearance made him the stuff of music folklore and he remains to this day one of rock's most enigmatic figures.

(•) Raver Timmi Magic claims that one unsuspecting driver left a service station on the M25 and was followed home by a mass convoy of illicit ravers, who thought they were heading for the next warehouse party; on seeing him pull up to his house, they confronted the unsuspecting driver, who invited them in. They stayed for two days.

(•) Robbie Williams' favourite drink is vodka and it is said his party trick is the ability to down four pints of Guinness in one go.

(•) Robbie Williams' 'Angels' is so well known that at live shows he almost always lets the audience sing all the lyrics.

(•) When Ramones drummer Tommy Ramone quit the band, he instead became a producer called Tommy Erdelyi.

(•) Seminal UK punk fanzine *Sniffin' Glue* closed down in February 1978, one month after The Sex Pistols split up.

(•) After a football injury failed to heal, Bob Marley had part of his right big toe removed.

(•) With the benefit of hindsight, Tom Robinson was a very brave man when he virtually billed himself as 'a self-confessed homosexual' and released 'Glad to be Gay' in the mid-to-late 70s. This was no mean feat given the homophobia present in the record industry – and society in general – in the 70s.

(•) Eurovison stats. The first British winner of Eurovison was Sandie Shaw. Three times as many women have won the contest as men. The first contest in 1956 was entered by only seven countries. Terry Wogan first commentated on the extravaganza in 1971. 'Nul points' was first recorded back in 1962 by *four* countries. The 1998 winner Dana International became the first transsexual to win, perhaps not surprisingly. Cliff Richard's 'Congratulations' in 1968 did *not* win. Norway's entry in 1994, 'Mrs Thompson', came complete with a full air guitar solo. Belgium's 'Urban Trad' cleverly got around the perennial language teaser of whether to sing in the native tongue or English by using instead a completely made-up language of their own – they came second.

(•) Henky Penky, the man who has tattooed some of the biggest rock stars in the world, including The Red Hot Chili Peppers, The Foo Fighters and The Ramones, is the son of a butcher.

(•) The Red Hot Chili Peppers have the following tattoos: Anthony Kiedis – two Maori designs, an eagle, daggers, two Indian chiefs, a stylised flower armband, broken heart, a tiger and the band's logo; John Frusciante – a pink octopus, band logo, a Native American Indian design, an Ornette Coleman design, an abstract image of a man and woman making love; Chad Smith – scorpion, eagle, Chinese characters and an octopus; Flea – picture of Jimi Hendrix, the name of his daughter, coloured elephants, an abstract, the word 'love' twice, an old Celtic design representing birth, death and eternity, his ex-wife's name Loesha, birds, a snake, dolphins and a Celtic dragon plus a tribal design from shoulder blade to shoulder blade. They did not have these done in one go.

(•) When guitarist Dave Navarro (Red Hot Chili Peppers, Jane's Addiction) was only fifteen, his mother and aunt were brutally murdered by his mother's boyfriend, a man whom Dave had loved like family. Dave was out of the house, but the man broke in and shot the sisters dead. An understandably unsettled Navarro later admitted to scraping the tastebuds off his tongue, just so he could look at them.

(•) Axl Rose cites Elton John, particularly on 'Bennie and the Jets', as his single biggest influence.

(•) Marilyn Manson has been ordained into the Church of Satan. Founder Dr Anton Szandor LaVey performed the ceremony and Manson, aka former music journalist Brian Warner, was re-christened Reverend Manson. His dad was a carpet salesman.

(•) Alice In Chains, stalwarts of the grunge movement, at one point boasted pillowcases, a music box and a wall clock among their official band-related merchandise.

(•) When Jerry Garcia of The Grateful Dead died in August 1995, San Francisco Mayor Frank Jordan ordered city flags to be lowered to half mast and a tie-dyed Dead flag to be placed on the City Hall's flagpole.

(•) When Prince/The Artist Formerly Known As Prince announced he would henceforth be called (symbol) 'squiggle', a Sydney, Australia radio station decided to run a competition offering the diminutive star some alternatives. Listeners chose 'Davo'.

((•)) The Maori chants sung by the New Zealand All Blacks rugby team are derived from the *haka*, a warlike dance accompanied by loud and fearsome shouting. Especially if it's Jona Lomu doing it. Maybe, on that fateful day when he almost single-handedly destroyed the English rugby team, his opponents would have been better per-forming the *poi*, a Maori dance involving gently swinging coloured beads around the head, normally reserved for women. That said, Maori tradition demands these songs are performed note-and-word-perfect, otherwise the performer risks some divine disaster.

((•)) Some Maori whistles are made from whale and shark teeth.

((•)) Traditional Mongolian music, descended from the nomadic tribes who traversed the Ural Mountains, consists of nasal tones meant to mimic animals, rain, wind and water.

((•)) Traditional Mongolian singers can sing a note and its natural harmonic at the same time.

((•)) The so-called 'Jew's harp' is played in Mongolian culture by holding the miniature instrument to the teeth and lips, yet it has no apparent connection with Jewish history whatsoever (although similar instruments can be found in the Amazon, tribal Africa and the Far East). Semantical discussions suggest it may be a misappropria-tion of 'jaw's harp'.

((•)) Paul McCartney's childhood home at 20 Forthlin Road, Allerton, Liverpool, is now owned by the National Trust.

(((•))) Björk's first hit was in Iceland, with a cover of Tina Charles' 1976 song 'I Love to Love'; the enigmatic Björk was just eleven at the time.

(((•))) Freddie Mercury's real name was Farok Bulsara. The surname was taken by Barry Bulsara, who was later convicted of killing TV presenter Jill Dando.

(((•))) During a lightning promotional tour of Brazil, at one point The Backstreet Boys opened their hotel curtains to find 45,000 screaming fans in the streets below.

(((•))) Songwriter Otis Blackwell's revered versatility led to a challenge from Al Stanton of Shalimar Publishing to write a song about a bottle of fizzy pop. Blackwell duly came up with 'All Shook Up', a Number 1 hit for Elvis Presley.

(((•))) Kurt Cobain is said to have purchased the gun with which he took his own life originally because of fears about trespassers at his home.

(((•))) Harry Babbitt, who died in 2004, was the voice behind Woody Woodpecker. However, he was also in the Kay Kyser big band from 1938 to 1949 and had hits such as 'White Cliffs of Dover'.

(((•))) According to *The Chambers Dictionary of Etymology*, edited by Robert K Barnhart, the term 'funk' is actually an intellectual word first recorded as Oxford University slang, and stretching back to 1677, where it is listed as 'a state of fear or panic'. The word probably comes from an old French word 'fonck', meaning 'agitation or distress'. It can also mean 'a strong smell', in particular the musty scent exuded by someone engaged in physically demanding sexual acts.

((•)) 'Punk' as a word stretches right back to the Algonquian tribe of Delaware, and – like 'funk' – dates from the mid-seventeenth century at least. The Native American word 'ponk' means, literally, 'living ashes'. The term was developed in usage to refer to any kind of small pile of rubbish, and thus to describe worthless items or nonsensical ideas. By 1869, and a story called *The Story of a Bad Boy* published in that year, the word had been coined to describe troublesome young hoodlums – the original punk kids.

((•)) Thus, the genre of music known as punk-funk (see The Red Hot Chili Peppers' earlier work) literally means 'a worthless kid who smells of the sex he has just had'.

((•)) On one late 90s tour, two groupie-wannabes managed to get into The Red Hot Chili Peppers' dressing room after a show, only to discover that the band had already left. The tour manager was there, however, wrapping up the night's work. They squealed at him and asked if the band had left any mementoes behind – he duly pointed out that a pair of bassist Flea's famous large white cotton Y-front underpants were in the corner on the (less than spotless) floor. To the tour manager's amazement, the two girls rushed to the pants, and the lucky winner grabbed them, screaming, before raising them above her mouth and wringing out a bead of dirty sweat into her throat. 'Now I have a piece of him in me forever,' she is said to have sighed.

((•)) Red Hot Chili Peppers guitarist John Frusciante's health suffered so badly during his heroin addiction that most of his teeth rotted away; subsequent surgery to replace them – using, among other things, bones from his hip – cost $70,000.

((•)) Eddie Cochran played all the instruments on both 'Summertime Blues' and 'C'mon Everybody'.

((•)) Nat King Cole was only 48 when he died of cancer.

((•)) A-Ha's breakthrough single 'Take on Me' hit the Number 1 spot in both the US and UK, selling millions of copies worldwide. In fact, it had previously been released – but without the seminal cartoon/live action video – and sold only three hundred copies.

((•)) Rock 'n' roll has offended the older generation since its inception – and prided itself on doing so. The first collection of music that might have needed a 'Parental Advisory' sticker dates from the thirteenth century, when a Bavarian monastery collated a group of songs about drinking, dancing and – 'Warning! Explicit Lyrics!' – sex.

((•)) On 17 February 1454, the Burgundian Duke Philip held a Feast of the Pheasant at Lille, during which guests ate from an enormous pie while 28 minstrels played music for their enjoyment – some scholars believe this to be the origin of the nursery rhyme 'Sing a Song of Sixpence'.

((•)) The first printed word came in the mid-fifteenth century with Germany's Gutenberg and England's Caxton vying for the claim of being the originator; musicians took up the new technology very quickly, the earliest sheet music of the modern world appearing around the turn of the sixteenth century.

((•)) Metallica's drummer, Lars Ulrich, was the son of a hippie jazz fanatic and club owner/critic. Consequently, Lars' childhood was filled with the sounds of jazz greats such as Django Reinhardt, Charlie Parker and Miles Davis. His father was also a professional tennis player, and initially Lars was a feared and promising young player too – until at one tournament someone gave him two tickets to a Deep Purple concert.

((•)) Metallica singer James Hetfield is the son of a Nebraskan trucker and an opera singer (his mother died when he was a teenager).

((•)) The preferred tipple of Metallica in their early days was said to be peppermint schnapps and vodka.

((•)) Metallica's bassist, Cliff Burton, was killed in a tour bus crash. His partner in the band, singer James Hetfield, had only moved from the bunk next to Cliff the night before because it felt 'uncomfortable'.

((•)) Famously hard-working Eddie Vedder (a one-time petrol pump attendant), lead singer of Pearl Jam, was already nicknamed locally 'the man who never sleeps', before he even joined the band.

((•)) When Pearl Jam's debut album *Ten* was released to muted applause in 1991, the band were told that sales of forty thousand globally would be a great start; then grunge happened and the album went on to shift more than ten million. In the midst of this spiralling success, the band played a free show at Magnusson Park, and picked up the entire bill for the show themselves, including an extensive free bus service, which ran to over $100,000.

((•)) Peter Buck and Michael Stipe of REM met each other while working at Wuxtry Records store in Georgia.

((•)) Pre-REM Michael Stipe briefly fronted a band called Gangster, dressed in suitable mafioso-style attire and singing an array of cover versions. When REM formed, they gigged so hard that at one point Peter Buck took to living in his Buick.

((•)) Many observers feel that the credit for early gangsta rap can go to Schoolly D, a Philadelphian rapper whose mid-80s records talked about how he got his money together, what he spent it on (Gucci watches and $200 sneakers, for example) and the colourful lifestyle that he enjoyed. In his classic track 'Saturday Night', even his silver-haired mother pulls a gun on him. Others suggest the origins lie with Niggers With Attitude (aka NWA), whose debut album, the classic *Straight Outta Compton*, contained a track called 'Gangsta Gangsta', which brought that downtrodden, neglected and highly stigmatised area of South Central Los Angeles into the lexicon of modern music.

((•)) When Ice-T (a former gang member who'd been releasing records only to small local acclaim in his LA home area) released the classic *OG: Original Gangster* album, he faced massive controversy with his track 'Cop Killer', which caused a stand-off with his label Time-Warner and pressure from the authorities, including then president George Bush, for him to back down. Later, when he was told to issue warning stickers on the front of his hard-hitting album *Rhyme Pays*, he printed them up in the shape of a bullet.

((•)) Rap pioneer KRS-ONE's stage name is an acronym for Knowledge Reigns Supreme Over Nearly Everyone.

((•)) Snoop Dogg (née Calvin Broadus) got his nickname from his parents, who explained that 'he had a lot of hair on his head as a baby and looked like a little dog.' The young Calvin's similarities with the famous Peanuts comic-strip character were striking enough for the nickname to stick. In the video for 'Who Am I (What's My Name)?' Snoop morphs into a dog.

((•)) Many fans of the gangsta rap lifestyle have been sent to serve time in the State Penitentiary in California. Snoop's cousin was sent there and was badly slashed in a fight. One in three inmates dies in there.

((•)) Snoop has a photograph of himself in his junior US football team taken when he was in his early teens, According to the rapper, '... of twenty-eight homies on the team, twelve are dead, seven are in the penitentiary, three are smoked out, and only me and Warren G are successful.'

((•)) Dr Dre is Warren G's brother.

((•)) Snoop Dogg is six foot five.

((•)) Seminal rapper Tupac Shakur was gunned down in Las Vegas and fatally wounded after a night out watching a Mike Tyson fight on 7 September 1996; he died one week later, aged 25, of respiratory failure brought on by his wounds.

((•)) Jazzman Albert Ayler's body was found in a New York river, giving rise to numerous conspiracy theories and rumours – one of which suggested his corpse had been tied to a jukebox.

((•)) When Ricky Martin played a US shopping mall show at the height of his 'Livin' La Vida Loca' fame, a helicopter had to be brought in to land on the top of the mall to fly him away from the ten thousand screaming fans who turned up, amid genuine fears for his own personal safety. Nowadays of course, if he started singing in JC Penney's, they'd need a helicopter that could carry ten thousand screaming people, for an entirely different reason.

((•)) As a youngster, angst rocker Alanis Morissette failed an audition for the internationally syndicated kids programme *You Can't Do That on Television* because she was too tall.

((•)) Glen Ballard, who co-wrote 'You Oughta Know' with Alanis, also wrote Michael Jackson's 'Man in the Mirror' – one of two hundred hit songs he has penned.

((•)) At the audition for Disney's *Mickey Mouse Club* TV show, an undiscovered Justin Timberlake was in the queue ahead of an equally unknown Britney Spears.

((•)) Karen Carpenter died of 'heart-beat irregularities', not from anorexia nervosa, albeit as a chemical imbalance brought about by the misleadingly titled 'slimmer's disease'. On a lighter note, The Carpenters were the only act ever asked to leave the grounds of Disneyland 'because they looked like hippies'.

((•)) In the late 80s, José Carreras successfully beat off leukaemia.

((•)) The Backstreet Boys' Brian Littrell was diagnosed with bacterial endocarditis aged only five. At the diagnosis, his parents were told, 'This illness has a 100 per cent fatality rate – go make your plans.'

((•)) The song 'Lili Marlene' must be one of the most treasured military songs of all time. Initially rejected by scores of German music publishers, on its release by the cabaret singer who made it famous – Lale Andersen – it still only sold seven hundred copies. However, it struck a chord with Second World War armies on both sides. Opposing forces were even known to *both* be singing it as they marched towards each other and possible death in no-man's-land. The 51st Highland Division is reputed to have launched an attack with one objective being to secure a copy; Hitler was so incensed that he reported the Allied adoption of the song as a breach of the Geneva Convention.

((•)) Rolf Harris is well known for his pop hits such as 'Two Little

Boys' and 'Tie Me Kangaroo Down, Sport'. He is less known for being the Junior Backstroke Champion of Australia in the 50s and for the exhibition of his paintings at the Royal Academy of Art in London way back in 1956.

(◉) The father of punk trio Blink 182's Mark Hoppus, Tex, is a renowned weapons engineer for the US Navy.

(◉) When promoting their album *Enema of the State* with a prestigious interview in *Rolling Stone*, Blink 182's Tom DeLonge opened the article with the words, 'Our favourite things in the world are pee-pee and doo-doo.'

(◉) Britney Spears shares her birthday – 2 December – with Peter Carl Goldmark, US inventor of the LP record.

(◉) Christina Aguilera's parents were a very colourful ethnic mix – her father, Jim, was from Ecuador and her mother, Shelley, was an Irish-American with German descent, who studied to become a Spanish translator.

(◉) As a young child, Eminem wanted to be a comic book artist.

(◉) During a spell of particularly bad luck, Eminem came up with his notorious alter ego, Slim Shady. The thunderbolt for his name and character actually came to him while he was on the toilet. 'So I wiped my ass, got up off the pot and, ah, went and called everybody I knew.'

(◉) 'Take me to the centre of everything.' What Madonna said to a New York taxi driver on arriving in the Big Apple to seek fame and fortune. She had $35 in her pocket – by 2004 she was said to be worth in excess of $350 million.

(◈) Madonna's Italian family come from a long line of farmers.

(◈) Madonna's famous behind-the-scenes video diary *In Bed with Madonna* was retitled *Truth or Dare* for the American market.

(◈) The Material Girl's highly controversial *Sex* book enjoyed a first print run of one million copies, half of which sold within five days of publication, despite the hefty $49.95 price tag. Madonna herself adopted the alter ego dominatrix name of Dita for the book.

(◈) Marilyn Manson denies the rumour that he had a rib bone removed so he could fellate himself.

(◈) US jazz trumpeter Cat Anderson won his nickname after beating up a bully at the orphanage where he was brought up. This is also where he learned to play the instrument that made him famous.

(◈) Among Justin Timberlake's nicknames at school were Brillo Pad and Pizza Face. Now it's the Trousersnake. For him at least, there is a God.

(◈) At the height of N*Sync's fame, that boy band even had lip balms produced as part of their merchandise empire – Justin's flavour was vanilla.

(◈) Westlife's promotional duties are the stuff of music biz legend. On one single day, the five Irish popsters were in five different European countries within the same 24-hour period. By the end of the long day, a disoriented Nicky had to ring his girlfriend, Georgina, on the mobile phone in the middle of the night to find out where he was.

(•) Although known for their ultra-twee pop music, two members of B*Witched first met each other at kickboxing classes.

(•) Celine Dion comes from a family of sixteen – her father Adhemar worked variously as a lumberjack, a butcher and a youth counsellor. The fourteen kids slept in four bedrooms and the entire family had only one bathroom. The young Celine was named after a song by Hugues Aufray that her mother was singing during pregnancy – 'Dis-Moi Celine' ('Call me Celine').

(•) Before he was a famous singer, Charles Aznavour wrote hit songs for Edith Piaf.

(•) Both Pete Ham and Tom Evans of UK group Badfinger hanged themselves.

(•) One evening in September 1969, while sitting at home in the UK, Eric Clapton received a call from John Lennon asking him to guest at a concert that was due to take place in Toronto – that evening! Eric thought it sounded challenging and so raced down to the airport, where he met Lennon. The pair headed out for Canada and rehearsed a few songs, including 'Cold Turkey', on the flight over, much to the bemusement of a jumbo jet full of passengers. A car met them at the airport and they drove straight to the gig, billed as The Toronto Rock and Roll Revival Show.

(•) Destiny's Child took their name from Beyoncé's mom, who was looking through the Bible reading the book of Isaiah, when the girls' picture fell out on a page that was discussing 'destiny'. So, it was, er, destiny. And Beyoncé was her, um, child. Clever stuff.

(◉) The title of The Strokes' debut album had proof-readers in a tizzy when they asked the question *Is This It* with no question mark; similarly, Oasis's album *Standing on the Shoulder of Giants* was pilloried for having so many giants but so few shoulders.

(◉) Barbara Erwin, the proud mother of Dixie Chicks Martie and Emily, was keen to encourage the early interest that her daughters showed in music, and studiously scheduled their singing sessions with an egg timer. Later, as part of promotion for their band, they published a twelve-page Dixie Chicks colouring book showing the perfect cowgirl style.

(◉) Shania Twain's parents were both killed instantly when their Chevy Suburban collided head-on with a logging truck. Shania – then called by her real name of Eileen Regina Edwards – looked after her three younger siblings by singing in bars and working day jobs too. So you might not like her music but you do need to doff your (cowboy) hat to her.

(◉) Plane crashes can be the blight of music stars' lives. Probably the first big casualty crash was the smash that took the lives of Buddy Holly, The Big Bopper and Ritchie Valens in February 1959; country music star Reba McIntyre lost all seven members of her band and her road manager in a crash; Ozzy Osbourne's guitarist Randy Rhoads died when a jovial stunt in a light aircraft went wrong; Patsy Cline died in a private plane in 1963 along with fellow country stars Lloyd 'Cowboy' Copas and Harold 'Hawkshaw' Hawkins; and more recently rising R&B superstar Aliyah was killed during a flight in between takes on a video shoot.

(◉) Enrique Iglesias is an avid reader of Ernest Hemingway. His favourite fruit is Spanish melons.

(◉) Julio Iglesias is reported to have slept with over one thousand women. Not all on the same night though, clearly. He also played in goal for Real Madrid. The original Golden Balls then.

(◉) Fiery Garbage lead singer Shirley Manson endured a tough childhood in the seedy back streets of Edinburgh. Her parents were an odd mix – a big band singer for a mother and a professor of animal genetics and poultry-breeder father.

(◉) Nirvana producer and Garbage drummer Butch Vig used to be in a band called Eclipse. The band's singer was called Worm, so called because of his penchant for eating the slimy creatures.

(◉) Butch Vig, Duke Erikson and Steve Marker used to record local bands at their Wisconsin Smart Studios. When acts didn't turn up, the trio would record under the name Rectal Drip – strictly only taping songs of less than sixty seconds and with at least one extreme tempo change. These three later joined forces with Shirley Manson to form Garbage.

(◉) Prior to 'Mmmbop' fame, the Hansons used to harmonise while saying grace at the family dinner table. I can just hear Sid Vicious turning in his grave…

(◉) The Animals' 'House of the Rising Sun' was inspired by a Bob Dylan version of the traditional song and recorded in fifteen minutes flat; the Tambourine Man himself took his idea for this song from a Woody Guthrie track but used a different key; Guthrie in turn found his inspiration for that version from a song that was popular in music circles at the turn of the 1900s.

(( )) Latino love sensation Jennifer Lopez named her debut multi-million-selling album *On The 6* after the subway she rode to her day job every day while still a struggling actress and singer/dancer. Just as well she chose not to live on the Upminster branch of the District Line.

(( )) A young Stevie Wonder used to spend so much time at New York's Apollo Theater that he would study backstage to keep up with the school curriculum.

(( )) One of the largest-ever government fines proposed against a US college radio was the $23,750 levied on University of New York at Cortland's WSUC-FM station for playing Kid Rock tracks such as 'Yo-Da-Lin in the Valley', an unashamed tribute to the joys of cunnilingus: It was initially stated that the fine was for airing 'obscene, indecent, or profane language by means of radio communication'. The charge was eventually dropped.

(( )) By the age of 21, Israeli Chaim Whitz had been an English teacher, a bodyguard, a jingle writer and even a typist at *Vogue*. Next up he changed his name to Gene Simmons and became the extravagantly tongued frontman of Kiss. Rumour had it that he had a cow's tongue implanted on to his own for effect (not that he needed to), and backstage groupie stories of what he could do with the said organ were the stuff of rock folklore. Notably, however, he and his band mates also once raised thousands of dollars for charity by selling 'kisses' with the band for 93 cents.

(( )) Part of the global Kiss merchandise empire in the Seventies included a Kiss lawnmower.

(( )) In November 1983, almost a third of the US *Billboard* Hot 100

chart were British acts, for the first time since the height of
Beatlemania: two tracks each from Asia, The Eurythmics and The
Police, plus songs by The Animals, Cliff Richard, David Bowie,
Elton John, The Kinks, The Moody Blues, Rod Stewart, Robert
Plant, Bonnie Tyler, Culture Club, Def Leppard, Elvis Costello, The
Fixx, Genesis, Human League, Jo Boxers, Madness, Naked Eyes,
Paul Young, Roman Holiday, Sheena Easton, Spandau Ballet and
Wham!. In 2003 and 2004, several weeks' US listings had *no* UK
acts at all.

((•)) Kiss released a full eighteen albums before removing their make-
up.

((•)) In reply to U2's album *War*, American soul and R&B band War
released a track called 'U2'.

((•)) Korn guitarist James Shaffer took up the six-string as a way to
rehabilitate a finger that had been chopped off near the tip in the
spokes of his three-wheeler bike. He was already called Munky
because his splayed-out feet looked like a monkey's hands.

((•)) Korn vocalist Jonathan Davis once worked at the mortuary of the
Kern County Coroner's office, as well as doing extra work as an
undertaker at funeral homes.

((•)) Jack Black, of Tenacious D, *High Fidelity* and *School of Rock*
fame, is the child of two rocket scientists.

((•)) At Woodstock II in 1999, the inflated food and drink prices ($12
per pizza, $4 per small bottle of water), and the appearance of cash
machines on site, fuelled an already tense atmosphere that ended in
mass riots. By the close of the weekend, there had been one death,

three weddings, 38 arrests (with more to follow), three thousand injuries, fiver trailers destroyed in arson attacks and a lot of exposed breasts, at a total cost of $38 million.

((•)) During the height of grunge, fashion designers started selling worn denim jackets *à la* the original thriftstore version worn by Pearl Jam's Eddie Vedder, labelled as 'frunge'.

((•)) Before helping to induct Neil Young into the Rock And Roll Hall Of Fame in Cleveland, Pearl Jam played a secret show billed as The Piss Bottle Men in Seattle's Moore Theater.

((•)) Radiohead's Thom Yorke was born with a lazy eye – Thom's early years were spent in and out of hospital, where doctors attempted without success to remedy his visual impediment. At one stage, a skin graft appeared to be on the verge of succeeding, but Thom's hopes were dashed when a bungled sixth operation left him with an eyelid permanently half shut.

((•)) From the hills and forests of Kenya, the Mau Mau group of revolutionary guerrillas rebelled against the British in the 50s until Kenya ultimately won its independence. Among the Mau Mau fighters was Ngethe Njoroge, who went on to become a Kenyan delegate to the United Nations – and father to Tommy Morello of Rage Against The Machine.

((•)) At one early REM gig, the solitary soundman went home, saying he was 'bored'.

((•)) Deke Leonard's real name is Roger Leonard. He renamed himself in honour of an Elvis film character, Deke Rivers.

((•)) Trip hop legend Tricky is actually called Adrian Thaws.

((•)) Ice Cube isn't an ice cube at all. His real name is O'Shea Jackson.

((•)) Seminal rapper Eazy-E was a former drug dealer who invested his money in a record label, Ruthless Records.

((•)) NWA received an official letter of warning from the FBI after releasing the watershed album *Straight Outta Compton* including the notorious track 'Fuck Tha Police'.

((•)) NWA's 1991 album *Efil4zaggin* has a title best read backwards.

((•)) When Eric Wright, aka Eazy-E formerly of NWA, was admitted to hospital in 1995, he thought he had asthma complications. He was instead informed he had the symptoms of the final stages of AIDS. He was dead within a month.

((•)) In 1998, workaholics Feeder played 115 shows in eight months including sixteen festivals over six tours in 66 major US cities across 45 US states, travelling 93,900 miles playing to approximately 484,000 people. One gig in Burlington, Vermont was played in an outside temperature of −14; another gig on the same tour in Las Vegas, Nevada had an outside temperature of 112.

((•)) Moby is a distant relative of Herman Melville, author of Moby Dick – he's his great-great-grandnephew. Moby originally went by the name of DJ Moby Deck.

((•)) Robert Smith of The Cure sings backing vocals on the first Associates album, *The Affectionate Punch*.

(◉) The most successful all-girl group in history in terms of record sales is neither The Spice Girls nor The Supremes. It is The Andrews Sisters, who sold over sixty million copies of their catalogue, including songs such as 'Boogie Woogie Bugle Boy'.

(◉) Little Richard's towering hairstyle, known as a 'conk', was so high that one observer remarked, 'there was almost as much of Little Richard above his neck as there was below it'.

(◉) Voice Of The Beehive didn't just name themselves after the famous haircut – they also wore them, joining the ranks of a cult hairstyle that is considered to be one of the tallest ever (and originally dating back to 1958). The band B-52's took their name from 60s slang for the beehive, which band members Cindy Wilson and Kate Pierson proudly sported.

(◉) Boy George once appeared on a US TV show called *Face the Nation* opposite a tele-evangelist.

(◉) When Bob Dylan said, 'Wouldn't it be great if we did something for our own farmers right here in America?' at Live Aid, the idea of Farm Aid was inadvertently born.

(◉) The first famous musician to succumb to an AIDS-related death was arguably Ricky Wilson of The B-52's.

(◉) When The Supremes enjoyed huge chart success and became the royalty of black US pop, some observers dubbed them the first 'Blaps', a rather crude abbreviation of 'Black American Princesses'. Their own towering haircuts were made more practical by a vast collection of stage wigs.

((•)) Twiggy the super-waif at the centre of Swinging London in the 60s, riding high on the popularity of The Beatles, the Rolling Stones et al., was also known as 'The Neasden Bambi'.

((•)) Brian Eno's full name is Brian Peter George St John le Baptiste de la Salle Eno.

((•)) Legendary designer and fashion guru Wayne Hemingway used to play saxophone in a band called Diversen, an indie/dance band in the style of A Certain Ratio.

((•)) Jackie Wilson, one of soul's finest voices, was attacked in his own home by a crazed fan called Juanita Jones. She shot him in the stomach and he was rushed to hospital where he spent two weeks recovering. The bullet, which had lodged in his intestine, was deemed harmless and it remained there for the rest of his life.

((•)) When The Undertones played Knock-na-Moe Castle Hotel, Omagh, during their 1980 Irish tour, the band's dressing room was just next to the hotel kitchen. When the band discovered this, they stuffed their hold-alls with frozen chickens and chips after the gig. Before they left, a reporter from the Belfast weekly *Sunday World* arrived and asked for an interview to shouts from bassist Mickey Bradley, 'I thought you were the great chicken detective!' Everyone roared with laughter and she left, minus her interview.

((•)) Vinicius De Moraes, who wrote the lyrics to 'The Girl from Ipanema', was also the Brazilian ambassador to Italy.

((•)) US jazz trumpeter and singer Chet Baker lost most of his teeth after being mugged in San Francisco.

(•)) The celebrated organist Paul Hofhaimer was famed for his travelling music shows, in which he performed on an ornate four-wheel carriage, complete with carved cherubs, which was pulled from town to town by a camel.

(•)) The most common song of the Bedouin tribes in the ancient Arab kingdoms was a so-called *huda*, sung by camel drivers and said to copy the sounds of a camel's feet.

(•)) Misinformed critics of Islam wrongly cite misogynistic tendencies in the culture. In fact, from very ancient times, women took a very prominent role in music and the playing of instruments in Islamic culture.

(•)) The Islamic instrument the *qanun* has 72 strings grouped in threes and is always played with a plectrum.

(•)) The Hammond organ is named after its inventor, Laurens Hammond, who launched it in 1935.

(•)) Robert Moog invented the Moog synthesizer in 1964. It was the world's first monophonic, analogue synthesizer made available to the public. Along with David Luce, eleven years later he invented the Polymoog, which was a polyphonic synthesizer.

(•)) The first synthesizer to use both a sampler and a computer was the Fairlight CMI, which came out in 1979.

(•)) A drum machine is simply a sequencer that is solely dedicated to percussion.

(•)) Nick Drake's initial shyness evolved into severe mental illness and depression. Some stories have the reclusive musician delivering tapes to his record company's reception before rushing off in case anyone recognised him. When his songs became more popular, he entered a psychiatric hospital and said he would never write music again. On leaving the hospital he got a job as a computer programmer (before his untimely death aged just 26 – possibly suicide, a theory denied by his family).

(•)) MIDI is an acronym for Musical Instrument Digital Interface, a sixteen-channel system that effectively allows musical instruments that come from different manufacturers to 'talk' to one another. The use of the word in musical recordings is different to its use for home entertainment systems that are described as 'midi hi-fi's'.

(•)) The sample rate of a sampler is the speed at which the machine takes 'audio snapshots', usually 44,100 per second.

(•)) A microphone is actually a 'transducer', converting mechanical energy into electrical energy. A vocalist's sound waves vibrate the microphone's diaphragm, and are then converted to the signal sent to speakers or a studio desk.

(•)) Martin Luther – the man who declared a rift with the Catholic Church that precipitated the Reformation, which subsequently altered the entire course of history – was also an accomplished flautist and singer who made a living as a young man by busking in the streets.

(•)) The word 'busker' comes either from the French for 'seek one's fortune' (*brusquer sa fortune*) or the Italian for 'prowl' (*boscare*).

(•)) The lute remains one of the toughest instruments to play, as this quote from sixteenth-century song composer John Dowland displays:

'Any lutenist who attains the age of eighty years must surely have spent sixty of them in the tuning of his instrument.'

(◎) Adam Faith was one of the very first artists to perform for inmates when he did a show in front of 'residents' of Leicester Prison in November 1961.

(◎) The legendary jazz singer Billie Holiday used to babysit for Billy Crystal, the actor.

(◎) Morrissey is hugely popular in, of all places, Mexico. Makes sense for a man who made his name singing about the grim urbanity of Manchester.

(◎) The inventor of the CD made the maximum length 74 minutes. His favourite piece of music was one of Beethoven's symphonies which was 74 minutes long – and he thought nothing should be longer than his favourite masterpiece.

(◎) Scooby Doo got his name after his creator listened to Frank Sinatra sing 'Strangers in the Night'. Ol' Blues Eyes starts off his scat at the end with 'Scooby doobie doo'. Don't think he mentioned Scrappy.

(◎) Norman 'Fatboy Slim' Cook was raised as a member of the Kosmon Faith.

(◎) 'The Jean Genie'/'Blockbuster' coincidence: in late 1972, David Bowie released the single 'The Jean Genie', a track he had written and recorded during his first tour of America. The rhythm was actually based on 'I'm a Man' by The Yardbirds, a band David had admired and often seen live in the 60s. At the same time, another glam-orientated band, The Sweet, released 'Blockbuster', a song they had coincidentally based on the same Yardbirds song. 'The Jean Genie' was all set to make Number 1 in the UK when it was perversely held back by Jimmy Osmond's 'Long Haired Lover from Liverpool' and then, ironically, by The Sweet's 'Blockbuster'. To add to the irony, both David Bowie and Sweet singles were released on RCA.

(((•))) Bowie, Bing and Bolan. In September 1977, David Bowie made a short visit to the UK to promote his new single 'Heroes'. Apart from appearing on *Top of the Pops* for the first time since 1972, David was booked to perform his new single on two TV shows, one with his old friend Marc Bolan and another with Bing Crosby on his annual Christmas Special. Tragically, within a few days of both recordings, both Marc Bolan and Bing Crosby were dead. Bolan died after his car hit a tree in south London and Crosby of natural causes while playing golf.

(((•))) Paul McCartney was reported to be the producer of the Bonzo Dog Doo-Dah Band's 'I'm the Urban Spaceman', credited as 'Apollo C Vermouth'.

(((•))) When Keith Emerson complained that his synthesizer was playing up, Lemmy stabbed it with a dagger he had on him. It fixed the problem, so Lemmy gave Keith his dagger... and, subsequently, the 'stabbing of the synth' became part of ELP's stage act.

(((•))) Lemmy taught Sid Vicious to play bass.

(((•))) On Lemmy's fiftieth birthday, Metallica played a surprise show for him at his local bar in LA – they played a set of Motörhead covers, for which all of them sported Lemmy hair and warts.

((•)) Lemmy used to be a roadie for Jimi Hendrix.

((•)) Motörhead were going to be called 'Bastard', though the managers insisted that they would never get any airplay, so the name was changed to 'Motörhead', a B-side of a single by Hawkwind (the band Lemmy was in before he was 'sacked for taking the wrong kind of drugs').

((•)) The father of Chicago-born Gil Scott-Heron – considered by many to be the godfather of hip-hop – played football for Glasgow Celtic.

((•)) Dave Dee – of Dave Dee, Dozy, Beaky, Mick and Tich – was a policeman prior to his pop career. As a copper he attended the crash in which Eddie Cochran died and Gene Vincent was severely injured.

((•)) The 'Echo' in Echo and The Bunnymen was a drum machine.

((•)) None of The Walker Brothers had the surname 'Walker'.

((•)) In the video of 'Dancing in the Dark', the young girl Bruce Springsteen pulls up on stage with him is a pre-*Friends* Courteney Cox.

((•)) Black Rebel Motorcycle Club was the name of Marlon Brando's bike gang in 50s movie *The Wild One*; Three Colours Red was one of a trilogy of European arthouse films (the others were Three Colours White and Three Colours Blue); Tairrie B's old band, Tura Satana, were named after an actress who frequently appeared in Russ Meyer films (his films include *Mudhoney*, from which the band of the same name took their name).

((•)) The Thompson Twins were named after the detectives in Tintin.

((•)) T'Pau were named after a Vulcan dignitary in *Star Trek*.

((•)) Mogwai are named after small furry things in the film *Gremlins*.

((•)) Duran Duran took their name from a character in the trash 60s sci-fi film *Barbarella* (and played their first gigs in a Birmingham club called Barbarella's).

((•)) *Coronation Street* has seen a cameo appearance by Graham Fellows, better known as Jilted John, and latterly performing as John Shuttleworth.

((•)) Steely Dan was the name of a dildo in the novel *The Naked Lunch*, by William Burroughs.

((•)) In 1976, totally against the prevailing punk atmosphere of the times, ZZ Top toured with a stage shaped like Texas, on which they placed a 2,000 lb fake buffalo, two turkey vultures and four rattlesnakes.

((•)) Keith Moon once bought a policeman's uniform and took to frisking his own band's audiences.

((•)) John Lennon's battles with US Immigration over his residency in America officially stemmed from a UK drug conviction, albeit only for marijuana. Conspiracy theorists, however, suggested President Nixon did not like his political leanings and ultra-high-profile platform.

((•)) Elkie Brooks was previously a singer in the band Vinegar Joe before going solo; one of her band mates was Robert Palmer.

((•)) Following 9/11, many US acts cancelled UK tours; this was not the first time this had happened. In January 1974, with the miners' strike and subsequent power cuts, several American acts also cancelled tours in Britain.

((•)) Performances of so-called *commedia dell' arte* – brief comedies acted by itinerant mavericks – were often accompanied by rudimentary music. One of the most popular characters in these sixteenth-century mini-plays was a hook-nosed prankster called Pulcinella, whose name has since been misappropriated for Mr Punch.

((•)) The Beatles' 'Yesterday' has been covered on record over 1,100 times.

((•)) Claude Debussy became one of the most popular music critics of his time – in complete anonymity. He hid behind the pseudonym of Monsieur Croche, meaning Mr Quaver.

((•)) The sixteenth century's finest English composer, Orlando Gibbons, enjoyed his highest acclaim for the work *Madrigals and Motetts* containing one piece, 'What is our Life?' which consisted of the poem written by Sir Walter Raleigh the night before his execution.

((•)) Rock 'n' roll has been witness to countless acts of sexual debauchery since its inception. Yet way back in the sixteenth century, overly amorous organist John Bull was lambasted by the then Archbishop of Canterbury thus: 'Bull has more music than honesty, and is as famous for the marring of virginity as he is for fingering of organs.'

(((•))) The song 'We are McIndoe's Army, We are his Guinea Pigs', released by the Royal Air Force, was actually a reference to the plastic surgeon who treated many of the airforce men disfigured by burns.

(((•))) Music legend has it that McCartney chewed vegetables on The Beach Boys' song 'Vegetables' (appropriately enough), recorded in April 1967.

(((•))) Two locations in the northern hemisphere have unique 60s rock connections. Swlbr, a volcanic island off Iceland, has no vowels in its name and is the name of a Cream song on *Disraeli Gears*; the other, Essaouira, a coastal town in Morocco, has all the vowels in its name and is the place where Hendrix wrote his *Axis Bold as Love* album.

(((•))) Serial killer Richard Ramirez said AC/DC's 1985 album *Fly on the Wall* had influenced him to carry out murder.

(((•))) Burt Bacharach (apparently) used to have a pet duck called Quack Quackarach.

(((•))) Wembley Arena was first opened in 1934 as the Empire Pool – and the 200-ft-long Olympic swimming pool still lies underneath the floor. During the war, the famous building was blacked out with 300 gallons of black paint.

(((•))) After Dunkirk, Wembley Arena was used as an emergency dispersal centre for thousands of ex-servicemen as well as a means of providing accommodation for refugees from France, Belgium, Holland and Gibraltar, even as events continued in the auditorium.

(((•))) The biggest selling male artist in the history of Wembley Arena is... Cliff Richard (52 shows!). Biggest selling female artist – Whitney

Houston (29 shows). Biggest selling rock band – Status Quo (38 shows). Biggest selling pop band – Steps (yes, Steps, 21 shows).

((•)) Korean War veteran and esteemed jazz baritone saxophonist Pepper Adams took up the instrument because it was the only one in the local music store he could afford.

((•)) Mike Nesmith's mother invented Tippex.

((•)) One of the earliest northern soul singers went by the name of Lenny Gamble, who released a passable version of Doris Troy's song 'I'll Do Anything'. Gamble was actually just a pseudonym for BBC Radio 1 DJ Tony Blackburn.

((•)) Joni Mitchell's first band was called The Saskatunes – a corny pun on the name of her hometown, Saskatoon, Saskatchewan.

((•)) Seminal DJ Alan Freed pleaded guilty to receiving bribes at a series of congressional hearings investigating the so-called 'payola' scandals of radio stations accepting money in return for airtime. He died before his trial opened.

((•)) With the popularity of 'pirate radio' stations anchored off the North Sea escalating, the UK authorities introduced the 1967 Marine Broadcasting Act, which effectively outlawed operations such as Radio Caroline. The BBC responded by forming Radio 1 and head-hunted many of the stars of such illicit stations, including John Peel.

((•)) Neil Young's dad, Scott Young, was a prominent sports writer and broadcaster in Toronto.

(◉) In the mid-60s, Neil Young and his band 'toured' Ontario in a 1949 Chevy hearse.

(◉) An unlikely fan of rockers Scorpion was Russian President Mikhail Gorbachev. He was so impressed with their Cold War ditty 'Wind of Change' that he even invited them to meet him at the Kremlin.

(◉) Radio Luxembourg closed down on 31 December 1991. It was, in fact, Europe's oldest radio station, having first broadcast in 1929 from Germany.

(◉) When Bill Drummond and Jimmy Cauty closed down their maverick band KLF, they recorded an answer-phone message at their office that said, 'Bill Drummond and Jimmy Cauty have now left the music business.'

(◉) Thrash metal gods Napalm Death have been known to play fifty songs in a twenty-minute-long set. One track, 'You Suffer', from their seminal album *Scum*, clocks in at less than a second.

(◉) A melody is a succession of notes of varying pitch. Unless you sing for a death metal band.

(◉) Interviewer to Napalm Death singer Barney: 'So how do you approach melodies?'
Barney: 'I don't use them.'

(◉) The first eight songs that Oxford band Ride released were the first eight they had ever written.

(◉) When Wet Wet Wet appeared on *Top of the Pops* to promote their Number 1 hit 'With a Little Help from My Friends' in May 1988, few people realised it was a double A-side with Billy Bragg.

(◉) Billy Bragg swapped a job as a bank messenger boy for that of driving a tank. As an aspiring musician he used to busk with two speaker cabinets wired to his guitar and perched on a home-made shelf across each shoulder.

(◉) The first ever double album is reported to be Bob Dylan's *Blonde on Blonde*, released in 1966.

(◉) In his very early days, Bob Dylan wore a black cap as his trademark look.

(◉) As a young singer, Bob Dylan went to New York to visit Woody Guthrie. He was spotted while there and signed to Columbia, and then put a tribute track, 'Song to Woody', on his subsequent eponymous debut album.

(◉) As kids, Sice and Martin Carr of The Boo Radleys used to practise getting off imaginary airplanes in readiness for when they were famous rock stars. As a seventeen-year-old, Carr was told by a doctor to stop his heavy drinking or risk a very premature death.

(◉) As a child, Mike Edwards of Jesus Jones used to babysit himself with his parent's record collection.

(◉) *Thriller* sold 40 million copies at approximately £10 a unit; *Sonic Hedgehog 2* sold 150 million units at approximately £45 each.

(◈) The Doors' 1968 album *Waiting for the Sun* was originally named after what the band believed was one of the record's strongest tracks. Before the record's release, however, the band had a change of heart and removed the song from the track listing, but kept the title.

(◈) There are only two artists in British chart history who have enjoyed twelve hit singles in the twelve months of a single year: Elvis and... The Wedding Present. David Gedge's influential guitar act achieved the unthinkable with their dozen single releases in 1992, each limited (by the band) to ten-thousand-copy pressings and only allowed one week in the charts before being deleted. In fact, Elvis' dozen included a couple of reissues from the previous year, whereas The Wedding Present released all new material; unlike The Wedding Present, Elvis did not film a separate video for each single, or issue a separate T-shirt range for each release either, as did Gedge and Co.

(◈) In his role as reporter for Dallas radio station WWR, John Peel (aka John Ravenscroft) arrived on the scene just after JFK's accused assassin, Lee Harvey Oswald, was killed in a police headquarters basement.

(◈) When Johnny Depp allegedly trashed his hotel room in 1994, The Who's Roger Daltrey reflected on the time it had taken and awarded him 2 out of 10: '[we] could've done the job in one minute.'

(◈) After his arrest for 'lewd behaviour' in a public convenience in Beverly Hills, part of George Michael's punishment was a fine of $810.

(◈) Geri Halliwell's first ever solo live vocal was the frankly rather embarrassing rendition of 'Happy Birthday' *à la* Marilyn Monroe, at Prince Charles' Fiftieth Birthday Royal Gala.

((•)) Prodigy manager Mike Champion previously worked in shipping.

((•)) Keith Flint from The Prodigy has one of modern rock's most dramatic hairstyles, with the shaved head leaving only two arcs of spiked hair above each ear; he wasn't the first to wear this style, however. Catwoman from the heyday of punk wore exactly this cut, and The Flock Of Seagulls' lead singer wore a similar two-pronged mullet, but flattened the remainder of his hair rather than shaving it off. It can be traced back even further than that – to a cut named 'The Banana Shingle Cut' in 1950.

((•)) One of the mainstays of the modern orchestra and classical music – the violin – was originally considered too vulgar for high society and was instead relegated to appearances at peasant dances.

((•)) Numero uno violin maker Antonio Stradivari made over one thousand instruments, not all of which were violins.

((•)) In sixteenth-century Italy, the latterday home of the opera diva, women were completely banned from singing on the stage or even in church choirs. As a result, a musical void existed for voices of a higher register. The so-called *castrato* male voice was used to fill this gap – unfortunately this was often created by the castration of young boys to avoid the deepening of the voice at puberty. To avoid awkward questions from the testicularly challenged boy as he grew older, excuses such as horse accidents or goose attacks were often given to explain his condition. This practice was even known to have occurred in the 1560s in the Sistine Chapel of Rome. Haydn was only prevented from such an operation the day before it was due, when his appalled father found out what was about to happen.

(•) Aphex Twin claims to only need two hours sleep a day, during which time he writes most of his music through 'lucid dreams', whereby he wakes up and the song is already written. It obviously works – he has a library of more than two thousand unreleased songs.

(•) The terrace cry of 'You Fat Bastard' was a compliment often thrown at so-called Jon Fat Beast, who compered at gigs by Carter the Unstoppable Sex Machine. He usually took to the stage wearing only a coffee cup over his genitals.

(•) Matt Johnson of The The fame taught himself all about the music business after reading an explanatory book written by Tony Hatch, songwriter behind the theme tune for *Neighbours*.

(•) Ian McCulloch of Echo and The Bunnymen fame met his artistic foil and fellow Bunnyman Will Sergeant while using the toilets of Eric's nightclub in Liverpool.

(•) In 1982, future Smiths guitarist Johnny Marr contributed music to a friend's band's song. The band was called Quango Quando and the producer for the day was Bernard Sumner of New Order and Joy Division fame.

(•) Bands who have used two bass guitars include Ned's Atomic Dustbin, Delta 5, The Logs and (occasionally) The Cure. Ned's Atomic Dustbin's debut album was called *God Fodder*, Black Country slang for 'good food'.

(•) Utah Saints were the very first band to be allowed to sample Kate Bush's voice.

(◉) On 26 August 1990, Stevie Ray Vaughan played a memorable gig at Alpine Valley, Wisconsin. The final number saw him duet on 'Sweet Home Chicago' with no less than Eric Clapton, Buddy Guy, Robert Cray and his brother Jimmie. That night, his chartered helicopter hit a three-hundred-foot hill, killing him and three of his tour party.

(◉) At least twenty songs have been released with a variant of the dance craze 'The Twist' in the title.

(◉) The Village People were Victor Willis (the original cop); Ray Simpson (his replacement); David Hodo (the builder); Glenn Hughes (the leather-clad macho-man); Alexander Briley (the GI); Randy Jones (the cowboy); and Felipe Rose (the Indian). These were not their real jobs.

(◉) Bandleader and trad jazz luminary Kenny Ball played at the wedding reception of Princess Diana and Prince Charles.

(◉) 'Hi-de-hi' may well bring back memories of the 70s TV sitcom of the same name set in a run-down British coastal holiday camp; in fact, the phrase was first used by bandleader Cab Calloway in the 30s and 40s as part of his scat- and impro-filled performances.

(◉) Chubby Checker did not write 'The Twist', he covered it; its creator was songwriter Hank Ballard. Chubby was discovered singing in a store while chicken-plucking. His name is a mimic of Fats Domino.

(◉) Ozzy Osbourne did not actually know he was biting the head off a real bat when one was thrown on stage once – he thought it was a fake rubber toy and sank his teeth into it as, er, a bit of fun.

((•)) When master composer Johann Sebastian Bach applied for a job as organist to a Leipzig church outside his native Saxony, the board of interviewers remained unaware of his reputation and unconvinced of his credentials. He only eventually got the job because the preferred candidate turned it down.

((•)) Bach's reputation at the time was not as lofty as it is today – many of his works have been lost, considered of no value. Indeed, manuscripts for six sonatas were discovered in a grocery shop as they were about to be used to wrap a customer's order of butter.

((•)) Although Elvis is widely criticised in some quarters for plundering black R&B, of the ten songs that appeared on his Sun singles, half had their roots in country & western; he was also a big fan of Italian *bel canto* singers such as Mario Lanza.

((•)) Between 1959 and 1964, rock music was said to have 'died' because Elvis joined the army, Buddy Holly died, Jerry Lee Lewis was banned, Little Richard went into a seminary and Chuck Berry went to prison.

((•)) Chuck Berry's seminal 'Maybellene' was first introduced into his live set as a novelty country & western song; he wrote 'No Particular Place to Go', aptly, while serving time for transporting an under-age white girl fan across state lines.

((•)) In his early days as a DJ, The Big Bopper held the world record for broadcasting non-stop, at 122 hours.

((•)) Jazz singer Cab Calloway, Little Richard, Annie Lennox, Kenny Everett and Shane McGowan were all born on Christmas Day.

(◉)) When Prodigy mastermind Liam Howlett was driving back from an illegal rave early one morning along the M25, he was overtaken by an ostrich. Assuming he had taken too many drugs, he continued home and went to bed bemused. He woke the next day to read about the bird, who had escaped from a local ostrich farm.

(◉)) The smell from a portable toilet at a festival is directly proportional to the sum of the square of the length of the queue and the quality of the food on sale.

(◉)) Cilla Black's real name is Priscilla White. She was once a cloak-room attendant at The Cavern Club.

(◉)) Clint Mansell, former frontman of grebo-rockers and all-round sample wizards Pop Will Eat Itself, went on to become one of Hollywood's most sought-after soundtrack writers, working on the blockbuster *Mission Impossible* franchise among other projects.

(◉)) The daughter of Coldplay's Chris Martin and Hollywood star Gwyneth Paltrow, Apple, is not actually a piece of fruit. Indeed, nor is Bob Geldof's daughter Peaches.

(◉)) Frank Zappa's daughter's full name is Moon Unit. She has never been to the moon.

(◉)) David Bowie's son is called Zowie. He was born in 1971 and now uses the name of Duncan in his chosen field of film production.

(◉)) Pete Tosh, the man who inspired the skanking black-and-white figure that became the logo of Two Tone Records, home to among others The Specials, was shot dead during a robbery at his home in Kingston on 11 September 1987.

((•)) Craig David appeared in the comedy TV show *Bo Selecta!* as a tribute act to himself called Craig Davies.

((•)) In the seminal musical film *Willy Wonka and the Chocolate Factory*, the advertising posters announced the maverick chocolatier's premises as 'everybody's non-pollutionary, anti-institutionary, pro-confectionery factory of fun'. Among the film's millions of devotees is Craig David, who took inspiration from it for his album *Born to Do It*. The band Veruca Salt also take their name from a girl in the movie.

((•)) For some years, rumour suggested that the part of Charlie Bucket, the impoverished child at the centre of the *Willy Wonka* storyline, was actually played in the film by a young Jon Bon Jovi. It isn't.

((•)) Only one of the children allowed into Willy Wonka's factory actually sings in the film – the greedy Veruca Salt, who delivers a loud rendition of 'I Want it Now'.

((•)) Flautist and French royalty Frederick the Great spoke French to his friends, English to his servants and German to his farm animals.

((•)) Bach died after going blind, having several unsuccessful unanaesthetised eye operations and finally being finished off by a stroke.

((•)) Sixteenth-century German musicians often met in coffee houses to play together, a culture dubbed *Collegia musica*. Sort of like a musical Starbucks. But without the mocha. Or the comfy seats.

((•)) Soul jazz pioneer Cannonball Adderley earned the nickname 'Cannibal' because of his vast appetite.

((•)) The 'Disco Sucks' movement reached its peak in America when thousands of people gathered at a football stadium to burn hundreds of disco vinyls in a pyre of glitter-ball-hating anger. DJ Steve Dahl invited his listeners to bring along their unwanted disco records to the baseball game at Comiskey Park between the Chicago White Sox and the Detroit Tigers. During half-time, one hundred thousand records were piled high and blown up with dynamite, after which a mini-riot ensued. The match was postponed and the White Sox forfeited the match. Although this might seem a little churlish and ineffectual, the campaign was later credited with accelerating disco's fall from grace.

((•)) Def Leppard's drummer Rick Allen lost his arm in a car crash, but rather than look for a replacement his band mates simply waited until he first designed, then made and finally learnt to play a kit specially customised for his disability.

((•)) U2's single 'The Fly', which topped the charts worldwide, was actually a demo.

((•)) Tenacious D, musical side project of Hollywood superstar Jack Black, are the self-proclaimed 'greatest band in the world'. To their fans, they are simply 'The D'. Likewise, The Grateful Dead are known by their followers as 'The Dead'. *Pop Stars* winners Hear'Say were widely known as 'The Shit'.

((•)) Concept albums are almost always rubbish.

((•)) After being refused their fee for playing a college gig in Nottingham, London thrash-punk band The Chocolate Speedway Riders accepted a lower offer of eight sets of cutlery from the union canteen.

((•)) When CDs were first introduced, manufacturers hailed their strength and resilience – one TV interview even showed a CD being spread with jam and then thrown across a room before being cleaned and then played in a stereo without a hitch. This was a claim which, as anyone who has ever sat and listened to a CD skipping its way into oblivion will know, was just a load of old marmalade.

((•)) Cliff Richard is the only artist to enjoy chart-topping singles in each of five separate decades.

((•)) In May 2004, a management agreement signed by The Beatles and Brian Epstein sold at auction for in excess of £122,000.

((•)) The first African star to be signed to a UK label was King Sunny Ade, foremost proponent of Juju music and owner of the rather splendid nickname Minister of Enjoyment.

((•)) Although Eurovision Song Contest winners Bucks Fizz are the butt of many TV show jokes, they can in fact boast eleven Top Twenty hits, including three Number 1s.

((•)) Christopher Lee, film veteran of more than 250 screen appearances, arch Dracula and Saruman in *The Lord of the Rings* trilogy, actually wanted to be an opera singer. He has an impressive baritone voice, a talent which ran in the family – his great-grandparents opened the first opera company in Australia.

((•)) The 2004 Number 1 hit 'Fuck It (I Don't Want You Back)' by Eamon contained the 'f' word 38 times; it was knocked from its perch at the top by the female riposte, the lovingly titled 'Fuck You Right Back', said to be by Eamon's ex-girlfriend, Frankee.

(((•))) Courtney Love's father, Hank, was a roadie for The Grateful Dead.

(((•))) A Justin Timberlake impostor masqueraded as the real thing during 2003 and even scammed his way into the so-called Trousersnake's own party in a top West End nightclub. The poser spent several hours mixing with the cream of UK celebrity until bouncers finally realised that he was not in fact Ms Spears' former beau and ejected him.

(((•))) At one point in the late 1600s, Rome officially banned opera.

(((•))) Handel collected art, including several pieces by Rembrandt.

(((•))) Early eighteenth-century examples of cellos were supported on the calf muscles by the crossing of the player's legs. Spikes to rest the instrument on the floor were a much later addition.

(((•))) Jogger's nipple is not exclusive to joggers. Female cellists get it too and it is a condition recognised by the British Medical Journal, no less. Perhaps that explains why most cellists are so bloody po-faced.

(((•))) Paradoxically, when Mozart wrote his symphony No. 39, famed for its exuberance and high spirits, he was desperately poor and in financial despair.

(((•))) Mozart was baptised Johannes Chrysostomus Wolfgangus Theophilus Mozart (try fitting that on a credit card). The first two names were taken after the saint on whose day he was born; Theophilus means 'lover of God'. In day-to-day use, Mozart called himself Wolfgang, but signed himself 'Amadé', the French version of Theophilus, although posterity has always used the Latin spelling Amadeus.

((•)) Rory Gallagher only ever played one main guitar, the beaten-up Fender Stratocaster with which he started his career in the 60s.

((•)) The soundtrack for the classic 1968 film *Planet of the Apes* consists exclusively of unusual sound effects. The man behind this innovative approach was legendary composer Jerry Goldsmith, who also composed the soundtracks for *Dr Kildare* and *The Omen*.

((•)) Although the very first US gold disc was presented to Glenn Miller for his version of 'Chattanooga Choo Choo', the very first million-selling record actually came 39 years earlier in 1903, namely Enrico Caruso's 'Vesti La Giubba'. Two years later, violinist Marie Hall was rewarded for her massive record sales with a gold bracelet decorated with seven tiny gold discs.

((•)) Elvis has been awarded the most US gold discs – 65; the Beatles are second with 59.

((•)) The US headquarters of A&M Records was on the same site as the movie studios once used for Charlie Chaplin films.

((•)) Berry Gordy set up Motown with only $700; when asked to describe his label in later years, Gordy said it was 'a combination of rats, roaches, love and guts.' He sold it in 1988 to MCA Inc. and Boston Ventures for a reported $61 million.

((•)) Herb Alpert and Jerry Moss set up A&M Records with less still, just $500.

((•)) Paul Abraham Dukas, the man behind the marvellous 'The Sorceror's Apprentice' in Disney's *Fantasia* film, repeatedly abandoned and often destroyed most of his work because of his own perfectionism. Only twelve pieces remained safe.

((•)) At their boy band peak, Duran Duran were nicknamed 'The Fab Five', which must make S Club 'The Shite Seven'.

((•)) Jim Lea wrote the tune to Slade's mega-Crimbo hit 'Merry Xmas Everybody' while in the shower; six months and 450,000 sales later, the song and his band were at Number 1.

((•)) Seminal guitar band Mega City Four played so many gigs in their early days from the back of their faithful van that they called an album *Tranzophobia* in its honour. Their lead singer Wiz earned his nickname not, as you may suspect, from any propensity for drugs, but for being a very swift winger in the school football team.

((•)) Elvis spent his last day on Earth having dental treatment then trying to get hold of a *Star Wars* print for Lisa Marie.

((•)) On his final tour, Elvis reportedly said the words 'I am and I was' under his breath so that only a few in the front rows of the audience could hear. Ever since his death, Elvis aficionados have debated what this could mean.

((•)) Thirteen US states have an official Elvis Presley Day; Alabama has an Elvis Week.

((•)) Elvis was blood type O.

((•)) The King's favourite meat dish was not a cheeseburger, but pork chops and gravy.

(((•))) Elvis' haircut is deemed highly influential in style and hairdressing circles, but it was actually copied from Tony Curtis – the King's previously blondish locks were greased and darkened into a duck-tail (or DA as it was known) after Presley saw Curtis with that hairstyle in the film *City Across the River*. When examined after his death, Elvis' hair underneath the dye was rumoured to be almost completely white.

(((•))) Soap operas do not just give us some of the most God-awful acting and unrealistic plot lines (which is why we love 'em), they have also given us countless examples of actors/actresses-turned-pop-stars, in an ongoing genre that should surely be dubbed 'don't give up the day job'. These include: Kylie Minogue, Jason Donovan, Robson Green, Jerome Flynn, Natalie Imbruglia, Danni Minogue, Holly Valance, Adam Ricketts, Jennifer Ellison, Martine McCutcheon, Tracy Shaw, Jack Duckworth and Ricky Butcher (don't tell me the last two aren't real people because I won't believe it).

(((•))) Ricky Martin is also a soap-star-turned-singer. He was the dashing Miguel Morez in the South American 'docu-drama' *General Hospital* before living la vida loca and becoming the biggest grossing Latin star in the world. Interestingly, he was the second pop success from that show, following in the footsteps of Rick Springfield (aka Dr Noah Drake), who had a smash hit with 'Jessie's Girl'.

(((•))) Film actors are not immune to the music bug either – those who have tried include Eddie Murphy, Bruce Willis, Keanu Reeves, Johnny Depp, John Travolta and Jennifer Lopez.

(((•))) Other unlikely thespians who also worked in music include Lauryn Hill, who may be a Grammy-winner of the highest credibility but once starred in *As the World Turns* before she joined The Fugees. Michael Damian, who starred in *The Young and the Restless*, later hit the airwaves with a cover of David Essex's 'Rock On' in the late 80s.

((•)) This glut of soap stars-turned-singers even provoked its own show. New York City music producer Donald Benjamin spotted the trend and launched the popular *Soap Sessions* compilation series, featuring stars of shows such as *Days of Our Lives* and *Passions* singing their own tunes, covers of past hits or holiday standards.

((•)) The wedding of Mexico's favourite pop and soap stars, Lucero Hogaza and Manuel Mijares, in 1997 was anything but private. Like a royal wedding, it was watched by millions of fans on TV and thousands outside the church itself. Even the Pope sent a message of congratulations from the Vatican, along with his blessing. Newspapers estimated the cost to the Televisa network – who opted not to interrupt proceedings with adverts – at $14 million.

((•)) The dashing star of *Dr Kildare*, actor Richard Chamberlain, released his vocal version of that hit show's theme tune, calling it 'Three Stars Shine Tonight', in May 1962. At the time, Chamberlain was receiving 3,500 fan mail letters *every day*.

((•)) The first British artist to top the Japanese charts was Helen Shapiro with 'You Don't Know Me' in March 1962.

((•)) Former merchant seaman Karl Denver was a hardnut Glaswegian who once spent thirty days in an Egyptian jail for hitting an Arab policeman. As a sixteen-year-old, he was already serving aboard a merchant vessel when he got drunk one night at a port in South Africa, fell down a gangway and broke his leg. While convalescing, he toured local tourist spots, heard a group of people singing 'Wimoweh' and thus came across his biggest chart hit (yes, it's the same song behind Tight Fit's Lyrca-clad success).

((•)) One of the oldest surviving and intact instruments is a silver trumpet found in the legendary tomb of the Egyptian Pharaoh Tutankhamen. As many of the archaeologists who discovered the tomb eventually met grisly and often unexplained deaths, there has not exactly been a rush to play this ancient trumpet.

((•)) Many folk songs originated as accompaniment to ease hard labour, such as rock breaking, digging fields or watching *Emmerdale*.

((•)) Although critics hailed Moby's 1999 album *Play* for its mining of 'lost' folk songs and melodies, interest in this sphere of music was in fact nothing new. Back in the 20s, the previously largely unheard folk music of the southern US states was collated together by one John Lomax on to record. Later, Ralph Peer spent years making field trips to these states to do more of the same.

((•)) Indian raga musicians are expected to improvise within a piece of music in exactly the same free-flowing manner that a jazz player would adopt.

((•)) According to the Dead Rock Stars Club website – 'The club all rock stars are dying to join' – the 80s saw the deaths of rock stars, pop icons and related people for some of the following reasons (all deaths from natural causes excluded): burnt to death, leukaemia, heart complications related to anorexia nervosa, acute tonsillitis, alcohol, cancer, heart attacks or related problems, brain tumours or haemorrhages, choking on own vomit while intoxicated, drowned, hacked to death, shot, murdered by beating, stabbed, car crash, motorcycle crash, plane crash, AIDS-related illnesses, drug overdoses, shot-

dismembered-and-dumped-in-a-canyon, emphysema, kidney failure, stroke, accidentally shot, exhaustion, bleeding ulcer, choked to death on a cherry pip, poisoned by floor polish and finally, falling down stairs after toppling off a chair changing a lightbulb.

((•)) Def Leppard Rick Allen was not the only one-armed musician to succeed – American Wingy Manone (Joseph Matthews Manone) made his name as a one-armed trumpeter. He composed 'Tar Paper Stomp' and even charted with 'Party Doll'.

((•)) Led Zeppelin drummer John 'Bonzo' Bonham was said to have drunk forty shots of vodka before asphyxiating on his own vomit in 1980.

((•)) According to a survey by *The Belfast Telegraph*, 825 parents questioned thought that pop stars and celebrities have a massive impact on what their children eat.

((•)) Britney Spears, fictional hero Harry Potter and rapper 50 Cent came ahead of the war in Iraq as Google's most popular searches of 2003 (in that order).

((•)) Busted were formed after bassist Matt Jay's karaoke rendition of Oasis' 'Don't Look Back in Anger' was seen by a manager.

((•)) The word karaoke is derived from the Japanese for 'empty orchestra'. Or 'empty pubs', by the time most lager-swilling pop-star-wannabes have finished.

((•)) R&B vocalist Shola Ama was discovered after a record company A&R man overheard her singing her way through a London underground station.

(●) Dairy products such as chocolate and cheese create phlegm and are avoided by many top singers.

(●) Janis Joplin ran away from home aged seventeen.

(●) When Janis Joplin died, she was working on an album called *Pearl*, which contained the song 'Buried Alive in the Blues'.

(●) The heroin found in Janis Joplin's body by the LA coroner was analysed and discovered to be ten times the purity of normal cut heroin.

(●) Vocal cords are two membranes within the larynx in the upper throat. When they are slack, air passes through them to and from the lungs; when they are tightened – i.e. when someone is singing – they vibrate, hence a sound is emitted. They beat together approximately 180 times a second. Within the head, along with the throat and mouth, the teeth, nose, neck and even sinuses all contribute to the sound created.

(●) The infamous 'nodules', so beloved as a reason for divas or rock stars to cancel tours, are actually severely painful and vocally crippling blisters on the vocal cords.

(●) The Ramones were the first band to have a video officially banned by MTV. Their promo clip contained images of hospital patients hallucinating and doctors dissecting skeletons.

(●) Pete Townshend's book publishing company was called Eel Pie Books.

(●) Toyah Wilcox played the lead role of Trafford Tanzi in the play of the same name at London's Mermaid Theatre in March 1983 – the same month that Blondie's Debbie Harry premiered in the same role on Broadway.

((•)) After performing over two hundred gigs a year for much of his career, former Deep Purple singer Ian Gillan was told to go a full nine months without singing a note or risk losing his voice altogether.

((•)) Gene Vincent died from a bleeding ulcer.

((•)) The Beach Boys' Carl Wilson steadfastly refused to fulfil his military service, stating that fighting in Vietnam was against his principles. He was threatened with prison before finally being fined $4,000 and put on probation for two years, during which time he was ordered to perform at prisons, hospitals and orphanages.

((•)) A gig featuring Jimi Hendrix, Eric Burdon and the band War is said to be one of the most prized bootlegs – it was recorded the night before Hendrix died.

((•)) Elvis' six-date tour in September 1970 was his first in the US for fourteen years.

((•)) Although Will Young was stuck in *Pop Idol*'s 'maybe' room for an entire day, when celebrity voice coach Cary Grant heard him sing, she leaned over to the show's producer and said, 'I think we've found your pop idol.'

((•)) When Darius Danesh asked an unimpressed *Pop Idol* panel of judges if he could sing one of his own compositions, he was flatly told 'no'. He had been intending to sing the song 'Colourblind' which, within a year, was at Number 1 in the charts.

((•)) Superstar Tom Cruise is a big fan of Glaswegian band Looper, brainchild of musician and celebrated novelist Stuart David and his wife Karn. Cruise was so enamoured with their records that he personally insisted on including their track 'Mondo 77' in the blockbuster film *Vanilla Sky*, where it can be heard twice: in the party scene and when Cruise's character is in his car, looking through some tapes, and says, 'What have we got here... We've got some Looper.' Stuart David's own robot also makes a cameo appearance in the movie.

((•)) Indie-weirdos Belle And Sebastian are known for being reclusive and even once sent out a 'band photo' that was a picture of a bicycle.

((•)) The Prodigy insist on using their own speakers and PA to supplement the house systems at the massive festivals they usually headline. This personal set-up cost £500,000.

((•)) Adam Ant once opined that gigging is the only way to improve, saying, 'There is no substitute for getting a bottle on the head at the wrong angle and having to keep singing.'

((•)) Andy Franks, one of the world's top tour managers, suffered a severe headache while on the road with Depeche Mode in Germany in 1987. Despite feeling severely ill, he was concerned for the security arrangements at the venue and worked through the entire gig in charge of the ten-thousand-seater show. He was finally persuaded to go to hospital for a check-up after five more days of partying (for which Depeche Mode are virtually unrivalled in their excess), only to be told he'd had a massive brain haemorrhage and should not have even got out of bed. A five-hour brain operation followed that left Franks partially blind, but he has since become even more sought-after as 'the man' on the road by becoming Robbie Williams' tour manager.

(•) 'Stand on the star. A verse and a chorus please.' What the *Pop Idol* panel of judges say to auditionees.

(•) *Pop Idol* finalist and Eurovision competitor Jessica Garlick had previously appeared on several TV shows, most music-related, but she also acted in a *Crimewatch* reconstruction.

(•) *Pop Idol* auditionees sing initially in front of the show's producers, not Simon Cowell et al.; if they pass, they are asked to go back three days later to sing in front of executive producers; if they pass that too, then they are sent straight in to Cowell's baptism of fire.

(•) One record company talent scout was famous for listening to the tapes he had been sent by wannabees in the car on his way home. He would listen to five seconds only of each tape and if it wasn't to his taste, it went out of the window.

(•) Blazin' Squad were discovered after recording a demo for a special price offer of £99 at the east London studio Xplosive; the producer on the day phoned up So Solid Crew's manager, a friend, and the band's career began.

(•) Macy Gray has been dubbed 'the bag lady of rock'.

(•) During the peak of Thin Lizzy's mid-70s success, singer Phil Lynott suffered from two separate bouts of hepatitis.

(•) A Phil Lynott imposter ran up large hotel bills in London by pretending to be the Thin Lizzy main man before it was spotted he had a tattoo on his left arm, which the genuine article did not.

((•)) Specials member Lynval Golding was slashed across the face and neck in a Coventry nightclub; the 'racially motivated' attack was perpetrated by both black and white youths. An admirably philosophical Golding said, 'I am sure the guys will feel sorry for what they did.'

((•)) Tex-Mex star Joe King Carrasco gatecrashed a Go-Go's sell-out Christmas party in only his birthday suit.

((•)) Prince and Bob Dylan both come from Minnesota.

((•)) Kirsty MacColl was the daughter of folk music legend Ewan MacColl.

((•)) Bob Marley's father was a British army captain from Liverpool called Norval Sinclair Marley.

((•)) Bob Marley was brought up in Trenchtown, one of the world's most poverty-stricken slums, in Kingston, Jamaica.

((•)) Bob Marley may have converted to the Rastafarian faith in 1966 after apparently seeing stigmata on the hands of the visiting Ethiopian king, Haile Selassie.

((•)) On his death from lung cancer and a brain tumour, Bob Marley was buried with full state honours in Jamaica.

((•)) Noel Gallagher was a roadie for Inspiral Carpets before joining his brother's band, Oasis.

((•)) Lewis Brian Hopkins-Jones of The Rolling Stones was a truant with two illegitimate children by the end of his teens. An an aspiring young musician he called himself Elmo Lewis.

(•)) Two days after their band colleague Brian Jones had died in a swimming pool (conspiracy theories about murder were refuted by the official verdict of Jones being 'under the influence of alcohol and drugs' at the time of his death), the rest of The Rolling Stones had to perform in front of 250,000 people at a free concert in London's Hyde Park. Mick Jagger read out a poem by Shelley in tribute to the recently deceased Stone and then released three thousand butterflies. Rather uncharitable reports suggested that most of the butterflies were dead, having been kept in airless cardboard boxes before the show.

(•)) At one early Bruce Springsteen club gig, the promoter walked on to the stage, pulled out a gun and shot one of Bruce's speakers. Then he walked up to Springsteen and whispered in his ear, 'I told you to turn it down.'

(•)) According to showbiz legend, several rock acts can claim to have killed birds that have flown in front of their speakers – the unsuspecting creatures all exploded from the ear-splitting vibrations.

(•)) It is a fact that Daniel Bedingfield wrote 'I Gotta Get Through This' in his bedroom on equipment that cost less than £1,000; multi-million-selling Prodigy maestro Liam Howlett recorded his first EP on a Roland W30 that cost only £900.

(•)) Former Babybird, solo star, novelist and film soundtrack wizard Stephen Jones issued his first five albums all on the same day.

(•)) When Radiohead performed their paean to suicide 'No Surprises' (a song about the destruction of one man's self-esteem, crushed under the wheels of his rat-race life) on *Top of the Pops*, the camera constantly panned across to the front row of the audience, to reveal teenage girls in boob tubes waving their arms from side to side. That's the magic of television.

(◉) Sample entries from the so-called 'Unofficial Rap Dictionary':
Benjamin – money, as used by Puff Daddy in his song 'All About the Benjamin'.
bucket – an old car in bad shape.
dap – a high-five style of handshake.

(◉) Artist requirements backstage, so-called 'riders', are the stuff of music biz legend. Peculiar requests have included: white drapes, curtain, sheets, chairs, flowers, tables candles and room (Jennifer Lopez); large pack of Skittles candy separated out by colour (Bloodhound Gang); a variety of local cheeses (Beck); 'no distinct smells near the artist' (Luciano Pavarotti); two bars of Dove soap (Destiny's Child); and a police escort if needed (Christina Aguilera).

(◉) Impressively, Frank Sinatra only usually demanded a clean room, sanitary toilet facilities, a mirror and dressing area, air-conditioning, some chairs and 'flowers would be appreciated'.

(◉) Jazz record company Blue Note advertises itself as 'the world's most sampled label'. Few could argue, with recent segments of its back catalogue being used by Gang Starr and US3.

(◉) An Italian scientist called Marconi achieved wireless communication in the late 1890s. Within ten years he was able to transmit signals across the Atlantic.

(◉) From the average-priced CD, 7.5% goes to the record company, 15% goes to the artist, packaging can account for up to 30%, retail outlet mark-up at least 30% and VAT adds another 17.5%.

(•)) A reverb pedal adds hundreds of delays – similar to the sound of a noise bouncing off a wall – to the original unprocessed notes.

(•)) A flange pedal thickens the input note by slowly oscillating an echo of the original.

(•)) The hiss heard when magnetic tape is used to record music is attributable to the randomly shaped unused parts of the tape, which produce white noise.

(•)) Digital data recording of music can store at least 1 to 2 million bits per second.

(•)) 'My plan was to synchronise the camera and the phonograph so as to record sounds when the pictures were made, and reproduce the two in harmony… We had the first of the so-called "talking pictures" in our laboratory thirty years ago.'
Thomas Edison, speaking in 1925.

(•)) Early recorded sound in cinema was very unpopular because audiences struggled to hear the phonograph.

(•)) In August 1926, Warner Brothers debuted the first Vitaphone film, *Don Juan*, which was the first mainstream movie that replaced the traditional use of a live orchestra or organ with a soundtrack, albeit with no dialogue.

(•)) The first movie with dialogue, or 'talkie', was *The Jazz Singer*, released in 1927. Although it was originally conceived as a singing picture with no dialogue, Al Jolson ad-libbed some dialogue on the set and the talkies were born. In 1928, *Lights of New York* was released by Warner Brothers as the first all-dialogue film.

(◈) In 1928, Disney's *Steamboat Willie* premiered. It was the first film to completely create a soundtrack in post-production including sound effects, music and dialogue.

(◈) In 1933, *King Kong* was released by RKO and made film sound history. Sound designer Murray Spivak is regarded as the first person to have manipulated sound for movie use. For example, Spivak used the sound of a lion's roar slowed down one octave for part of Kong's roar – a trick later used along with other sound effects for scores of ultra-modern hi-tech films, such as *Jurassic Park*.

(◈) The car Marc Bolan died in was a purple Mini 1275 GT; it had been serviced only three days earlier, the only major repairs being a new tyre and the then standard balancing of the wheels.

(◈) Marc Bolan played guitar on David Bowie's 'The Prettiest Star'.

(◈) Marc Bolan wrote as a guest columnist for *Record Mirror* for a short time.

(◈) In 1940, Walt Disney's *Fantasia* was released. Recording began on 7 April 1939, and consumed half a million feet of sound film during 42 days of recording.

(◈) On 30 September 1952, the film *This is Cinerama* premiered as the debut Cinerama film. Cinerama was the first real widescreen feature-film format and was invented by Fred Waller. It is also the name of former Wedding Present frontman David Gedge's next band.

(◈) The father of Damon Albarn, lead singer of Blur, comes from a long line of Lincolnshire Quakers. Damon's grandfather had served time during the Second World War for his conscientious objection.

His mother's parents were farmers who accommodated prisoners of war to work on their land during the conflict. Damon's father was an artist who also presented a BBC2 arts show that became the pilot production for *The South Bank Show*.

(♦)) Damon Albarn's mother was an accomplished stage designer who worked for the revolutionary Theatre Royal Stratford East company of Joan Littlewood. She worked on many productions, including one, *Mrs Wilson's Diary*, while pregnant with Damon.

(♦)) The word 'orchestra' comes from the Greek word used to describe the front area of a stage in classical theatre.

(♦)) The pointy thing that an orchestra's conductor holds is called a baton. The eccentric conductor Louis Jullien owned a bejewelled pointy thing that was handed to him at the start of each performance on a silver platter.

(♦)) In the early nineteenth century, most orchestras contained 35 musicians; by the early twentieth century, the average figure had swelled to 70.

(♦)) Mozart struggled to maintain the celebrity and lucrative career he had enjoyed as a child prodigy. He wrote of one poorly paid royal post that his salary was 'too much for what I am asked to do, too little for what I could do'.

(♦)) Most people forget that Yoko Ono was a highly acclaimed and controversial conceptual artist of ten years' standing in her own right before she met her future Beatle husband. Her 1966 London exhibition asked people to 'communicate with the other members by mental telepathy'.

((•)) At one of Blur's earliest gigs, when they were still called Seymour, a night of especially copious drinking followed a show of Goldsmiths students' work – bassist Alex woke up early the next morning in the middle of a field in Kent, while Damon blacked out after two bottles of tequila and fell asleep in Euston station. The police saved him from some tramps and slung him in Holborn police cells to sober up; he was brought round by a Nepalese soldier in full uniform. The tramps had stolen all his money so he had to walk home.

((•)) The Cranberries initially spelt their name Cranberry's.

((•)) In 1985, Kurt Cobain worked as a lifeguard at a YMCA.

((•)) Kurt Cobain first met future wife Courtney Love at a Butthole Surfers show.

((•)) Nirvana's *Nevermind* album initially charted at only Number 144 in the US *Billboard* listings; later the next year, the record toppled Michael Jackson's *Dangerous* from the Number 1 spot.

((•)) The final Nirvana show was played in Munich, in March 1994. Two days later, Cobain was hospitalised comatose, after overdosing on Rohypnol and champagne. When he awoke from twenty hours in a coma, he asked for a milkshake. Three days later, he shot himself dead.

((•)) Manic Street Preacher Nicky Wire (born Jones) once said, 'If you built a museum to represent [his hometown of] Blackwood all you could put in it would be shit, rubble and shit.'

((•)) The first record James Bradfield, lead singer of Manic Street Preachers, bought was Diana Ross' 'My Old Piano'.

(((•))) When Beethoven reached thirty, he began to have trouble with his hearing and eventually had the worst fate of all for a composer – he went deaf. Similarly, James Hetfield of Metallica suffers from severe tinnitus. Can't think why.

(((•))) Beethoven's Third Symphony was originally dedicated to Napoleon Bonaparte, for whom the composer had great admiration. However, when Napoleon crowned himself Emperor and proceeded to betray many of his earlier revolutionary ideals, Beethoven deleted – by hand – the dedication on the first page of the score and replaced it simply with the word 'Eroica' (heroic).

(((•))) Although it was considered a fashionable haircut at the time, Mozart had a right mullet.

(((•))) In 1977 Marc Bolan died in a car crash; in 1980 Tyrannosaurus Rex's Steve Peregrin Took spent a royalty cheque on magic mushrooms and later choked on a cherry; then, in 1981, the band's bassist during their most successful years, Steve Currie, died in another car crash, this time in Portugal.

(((•))) The album title *Double Nickels on the Dime* used by hardcore exponents The Minutemen is trucker lingo for travelling at 55 mph on the American Interstate 10 highway.

(((•))) Songwriter and cult hero Tim Buckley died in June 1975 from what was described as 'an overdose of heroin and morphine'. However, rock music rumour suggests he may have died accidentally after mistaking a line of white powder for cocaine. His son, Jeff, with whom he had no tangible relationship ('I knew [him] for a total of nine days,' Jeff once stated), drowned in May 1997 after taking a swim in the Mississippi fully clothed.

(•)) Joy Division took their name from the prostitution wing of a concentration camp.

(•)) 'We look like nothing else on earth. A car bomb kiss off to The Face. Politics and adolescent cheap sex. Fuck the rotten edifice of Manchester. Too safe in dressing like a bricklayer. Too boring. Too macho, males afraid of themselves.'
Extract from a letter sent by Manic Street Preachers to *NME*, one of several hundred individual letters they wrote out by hand before they had even recorded one song.

(•)) When Richey Edwards, former guitarist of Manic Street Preachers, vanished in February 1995, he left behind his passport, a bottle of Prozac and his credit cards on his unmade bed. Reported sightings have placed him as far afield as India but seven years later his missing persons report was changed to 'presumed dead'.

(•)) Richard Melville Hall, aka Moby, calls himself 'The Little Idiot'.

(•)) Francis Grasso – resident DJ at New York's infamously debauched club Sanctuary, a disused church in the tough Hell's Kitchen district – was the first DJ to segue records into one seamless, uninterrupted mix.

(•)) Walter Gibbons, resident DJ at Galaxy 21 in New York, was the first DJ to add a live drummer to beef up his record spinning – he chose Francois Kervokian as his sticksman, who later became a renowned DJ himself.

(•)) Hardcore music is also known by some observers as 'bleep and bass'.

((●)) Although not all of the offers came to fruition, within the same twelve-hour period of one day in 1999, Moby was asked to produce Guns N' Roses, work with John Lydon and write material for the new James Bond movie (he did the last two).

((●)) The KLF have produced some of the rock business's greatest publicity stunts and bizarre events. They famously burnt £1 million in cash and wrote a book about how to have a Number 1 hit.

((●)) Ravi Shankar is probably the best-known Indian musician of the modern era – at least in the Western world. He has a brother, Uday, who is considered one of the finest proponents of the marriage between Indian classical dance and modern Western ballet.

((●)) The colourful African-rumba rock star Papa Wemba was born to a mother who was a 'wailer' at funerals. Her son's style is renowned for being compulsively melancholy.

((●)) Youssou N'Dour, who famously worked with Paul Simon on the multi-million-selling album *Gracelands*, is a direct blood descendant of travelling African minstrels.

((●)) A 'cakewalk' is an early form of African-American dance.

((●)) In the summer of 1980, Dexy's Midnight Runners took out full page adverts in the music press to announce they would never again be interviewed by the music media; instead of talking to the 'dishonest, hippy press', they would issue more adverts containing their own adverts and essays.

((●)) At The Specials' US debut gig, singer Terry Hall announced, 'We just can't say how pleased you must be to have us here ...'

(•) When thousands of fans arrived early for The Who's gig at the Riverfront Coliseum in Cincinnati on their 'comeback' tour, an ensuing crush killed eleven people. The Who played the gig nonetheless, unaware of the tragedy – the local police feared a violent riot if the show was cancelled.

(•) When super-hippy-disco-soul band Earth, Wind and Fire played Madison Square Gardens in 1979, fifteen fans were arrested for mugging.

(•) Jethro Tull's Ian Anderson was once hit in the eye by a rose thrown from the audience. That's some shot...

(•) The term Dixieland, used to describe traditional jazz styles, derives from Jonathan Dixie, an American slave trader.

(•) Second World War singers The Beverley Sisters were still together in 2004 and therefore able to give a concert of old-time songs for five hundred war veterans at the D-Day celebrations in Portsmouth.

(•) Les Pattinson of Echo and the Bunnymen is also a boat-builder and sand blaster.

(•) Ian McCulloch, not known for his modesty, once famously said, 'It's hard work being a 24-hours-a-day soddin' icon.'

(•) A sixteen-year-old pre-Primal Scream Bobbie Gillespie used to play in an ad hoc band with a friend called Jim Beattie that used to rehearse in the local scout hall, playing what amounted to little more than untrained white noise. They even used an old ventilator and a couple of dustbin lids.

((•)) Pulp took fourteen years to record what they called their 'debut' album.

((•)) Modern Algerian music is best exemplified by the style known as 'Rai'.

((•)) Jarvis Cocker is admired and fawned over for his 'charity shop chic'. Yet, when he was a young boy, he was the very opposite of a fashion icon. After a grave bout of meningitis had left his eyesight severely impaired when he was only five, he had to wear the thick-framed NHS spectacles that were the bane of every short-sighted 70s school kid. To make matters worse, his loving mother dressed him in ridiculous leather shorts bought by a relative and, with his long hair, bad teeth and angular bottle-top glasses, Jarvis was an obvious target for school bullies.

((•)) The word 'psychedelia' was first used in San Francisco in 1965.

((•)) George Harrison bought his first sitar in 1965.

((•)) Possibly the first ever soul record was Ray Charles' 'I Gotta Woman', which combined his gospel-inflected vocals with lyrics drawn straight from R&B.

((•)) While his sister Karen struggled, and ultimately failed, to beat anorexia nervosa, Richard Carpenter sought treatment for addiction to Quaaludes – all something of a shock for a band whose squeaky-clean, wholesome image had made them America's, and indeed the world's, favourite duo.

((•)) The Byrds songwriter Gene Clark suffered from both severe stage fright and a fear of flying – not ideal if you want to be a rock star.

((•)) One evening in 1985, Jarvis Cocker was at a party trying to impress a girl by hanging off a window ledge. Jim Morrison did it, Keith Moon did it, so did Iggy. Unfortunately, Jarvis was none of these and fell three floors to the ground, smashing his pelvis, wrist and foot and suffering severe internal bruising as a result. A six-week spell in a hospital ward full of old miners ensued, followed by a further two months in a wheelchair.

((•)) By the time The Sex Pistols were touring the USA, Sid Vicious' drug habit was so severe that legend has it that he had to be woken up from his stupors with a cattle prod, originally bought after receiving death threats. At some gigs he was gaffer-taped to the speaker cabinet to prevent him falling over. At the Dallas Longhorn Ballroom three of his four bass strings were broken but he did not notice.

((•)) At a press conference for the Pistols' rather brilliant reunion gigs in 1996, John Lydon said, 'Sid actually did nothing. Sid was a coathanger.'

((•)) At one early Clash gig, a group of ten large, beer-swilling heavy metal fans were baiting the band and heckling them incessantly. Suddenly Sid Vicious ran across from the back of the stage, past the members of The Clash, and launched himself into the air and out on to the heads of these metal fans. After the initial advantage of surprise had worn off, however, Sid was beaten ferociously.

((•)) With The Sex Pistols' *Never Mind the Bollocks* album barely scraping into the bottom of the *Billboard* Top 100 in 1977, America seemed wary of the coming tour – one southern reporter claimed they broke hamsters in half on stage.

(◉) Fats Domino was playing R&B to great success throughout the 50s, but when rock 'n' roll appeared, he was immediately dubbed a leader of this new genre by the rather ill-informed media.

(◉) Rumour has it that early DJ Alan Freed tried to copyright the term 'rock 'n' roll'.

(◉) Kelly Jones and Stuart Cable of the Stereophonics lived eight doors apart on the same street in the Welsh former pit village of Cwmaman; third member Richard Jones's house was reached by crossing a football pitch.

(◉) When a then up-and-coming Supergrass played at EMI's annual conference in Brighton, the band's drummer Danny Goffey, clad in loon pants and a woolly jumper, spotted the pop royalty that is squeaky-clean Sir Cliff Richard. He went across, shook Cliff's hand and said, 'All right man, how are you? I'm sorry, I don't understand what's going on – I'm on acid.' On being told Supergrass had just released their debut single and that the singer Gaz was still only eighteen, Cliff rightly pointed out that he had put out his first record when still aged seventeen. Supergrass' vocalist quickly retorted, 'Yeah, but I bet it wasn't about smoking drugs.'

(◉) The mother of Coldplay drummer Will Champion was being buried the day before the band recorded the video for their breakthrough single, 'Yellow', so it was left to singer Chris Martin to film the footage alone; he attributes the solemn mood of the shot of him walking across a beach to this sad news.

(◉) On the album cover of the 15-million-selling record *Tragic Kingdom*, No Doubt lead singer Gwen Stefani is wearing a dress that cost $14.

((•)) Gwen Stefani married her rock star husband Gavin Rossdale of the UK band Bush twice – once in London and once in LA. For the UK ceremony she kept him on tenterhooks for ninety minutes.

((•)) Original AC/DC singer Bon Scott was in fact a Scot by birth and was deemed 'socially maladjusted' by the army of his adopted country, Australia.

((•)) The Plasmatics' Wendy O usually took to the stage with little more than bondage knickers and shaving cream or tape over her nipples. She appeared in an episode of *McGyver* and went on to become a devotee of healthy eating and fitness, before killing herself aged 48.

((•)) Young Canadian crooner Michael Buble was a singing telegram before hitting the big time. He once received a teddy bear from a female fan and was about to give it to his nephew when he noticed the 'Press me' sticker on the paw. He did so and the bear said, in the female fan's voice, 'Hi, my name's Henrietta, I want to touch you, I'm staying at this hotel…'

((•)) Extreme jazz purists maintain that the very nucleus, the core spirit of the genre, is improvisation, and they therefore wholly reject any transcription or written scores.

((•)) Although the Moog and then MiniMoog are seen as watershed inventions in the history of electronic music, the Sequential Circus Prophet 5 was a less-lauded but equally sizeable breakthrough: it could play five notes simultaneously and had a memory.

((•)) The first widely available commercial analogue drum machine was the Roland Tr-808 – from which techno act 808 State derived their name.

((•)) Billie Holiday sang with some of the finest white musicians of the Second World War era. However, when each performance was complete, she would usually be segregated from her white colleagues on different trains, hotels and buses.

((•)) Drummer Pete de Freitas replaced the drum machine 'Echo' in Echo and the Bunnymen, only to be later killed in a motorbike accident in 1989. Before he died, and contrary to the Bunnymen's otherwise fairly un-noteworthy rock lifestyle, De Freitas is said to have been on one of rock's biggest ever benders, during which he is reported to have stayed awake for *eighteen days*.

((•)) The word 'crooner' was originally used to describe singers who used the very first microphones and found that, instead of having to sing unamplified and therefore at a certain volume, they could sing at any level they wanted. Naturally, they took advantage of this to sing more quietly at times, creating a more intimate mood – thus crooning was born.

((•)) The technological development that sent the guitar into the stratosphere as a global cultural icon came in the 30s with the advent of electrification. Blues and jazz players were among the first to recognise the potential this offered, not least because the previously quiet acoustic guitar could now be replaced with one that could easily be heard over the loud fanfares of the brass sections in bands.

((•)) David Beckham, husband of Posh Spice Victoria, shares the same birthday, 2 May, as the author's wife. Now stop nagging me, woman.

((•)) In the last week of May 2004, US R&B artist Usher had three singles in the US Top Ten – a feat only previously matched by The

Beatles and The Bee Gees. His hits were: 'Burn' (1); 'Yeah!' (4); 'Confessions Part II' (9).

(•) In the half-time interval of the 2004 American Football Superbowl, during a performance with Justin Timberlake, Janet Jackson's jacket fell away from her body revealing a naked breast and a bejewelled nipple ring. After mass outrage, including threatened lawsuits for supposedly 'false advertising' (the Superbowl is a family day in the US), Janet explained away the 'error' as 'a wardrobe malfunction'. Bizarrely, she later implied that the furore was actually engineered by shadowy establishment figures, whom she referred to only as 'they', by way of distracting the world from the Iraq war. Right.

(•) By May 2004, Elvis Presley had spent more time in the UK charts (47 years, two months) than he did alive.

(•) After appearing in a promo video as 'Bin Shady', an Osama bin Laden spoof, Eminem received several death threats from extremist groups.

(•) Britney Spears, Madonna, Posh Spice and Jerry Hall are all said to be followers of what some cynics have unfairly dubbed the so-called 'celebrity religion', Kabbalah. The beloved prophet behind this religion, Feivel Gruberger, was actually an insurance salesman.

(•) The initial report into the death of Toto drummer Jeff Porcaro said he had died of an allergic reaction to lawn pesticide; it later transpired it was a hardening of arteries caused by cocaine abuse.

(•) Robbie Williams' first ever solo show in the US was in front of one hundred invited guests at the aptly-named Phoenix Hotel in LA.

After the performance, he said, 'Thank you very much, if you've enjoyed me, my name is Robbie Williams; if not, then my name is George Michael.'

((•)) The white stripe on hip-hop superstar Nelly's cheek is an on-going mark of respect to an imprisoned family member.

((•)) Chrissie Hynde worked in Malcolm McLaren's Sex clothes shop and also wrote reviews for *NME* before hitting it big with The Pretenders.

((•)) When Russian pop duo Tatu shot to Number 1 with the song 'All the Things She Said' – accompanied by a highly controversial video in which they starred as schoolgirls snogging by a frankly rather unpleasant and wet old fence – the moral majority were outraged. Playing on this, the duo and their Svengali-like manager announced that the girls were in fact lovers in real life. Cue more hysteria. The follow-up songs failed to match the duo's earlier dizzy heights, however, and public interest waned, being finally extinguished when it emerged that one half of the duo, Julia Volkova, was pregnant by a long-term boyfriend.

((•)) Actor Gary Oldman, star of the punk movie *Sid and Nancy* among many other acclaimed big-screen appearances, recently taught Harry Potter to play bass. Well, not Harry Potter as such, but Daniel Radcliffe, who was starring in the title role alongside Oldman (who played the part of Sirius Black, Harry's godfather) in the third movie in the series, *Harry Potter and the Prisoner of Azkaban*.

((•)) In the fifth Harry Potter book, *Harry Potter and the Order of the Phoenix*, Sirius Black is alleged to have not been a murderer after all; instead, it is claimed in a tabloid red-top called *The Quibbler* that he was in fact in a band, 'the popular singing group The Hobgoblins', and was sharing a romantic candle-lit dinner with a groupie fan at the time of his alleged crimes.

(•) The Munchkins who starred in *The Wizard of Oz* were actually the so-called 'Singer Midgets', named after the German who found and 'trained' them as acrobats, singers, dancers and wrestlers. They were said to have received less than $100 a week for their work.

(•) For the early musical film *Singin' in the Rain*, hidden microphones were placed in the oddest places, including in a plant pot, on Lina Lamont's corset at the breast and also on her shoulder. At one point, Lamont's necklace can be heard jangling very close to the mike.

(•) In 1929, when sound technology was still stumbling along, Bebe Daniels, the star of the film *Rio Rita* had to open a paper fan – however, the fan made such a rustling noise, 'like a thunderstorm', that it had to be remade in (quieter) silk to look like paper.

(•) In the late 60s, Radio Luxembourg was the only European station that played American rock 'n' roll.

(•) A 1961 radio made by Roberts is now considered a design classic and costs £120.

(•) George Harrison's 'Let it Be' guitar was so-named because he used it for the album of that name. The six-string was actually a Fender Rosewood Telecaster – the same instrument he used to perform on the roof of Apple Records when The Beatles caused a stir there in January 1969 (incidentally their last public performance). He originally paid a retail price of $395 for it; the same guitar sold on eBay in 2003 for $434,750.

(◈)) John Lennon's remarkable 1965 Rolls-Royce Phantom V, painted in gaudy psychedelic patterns on his instruction by a team of gypsy artists, sold in 1985 at Sotheby's in Manhattan for $2.3 million – compared to the cost of a 'standard' Phantom V in that year of approximately £35,000. The buyer was rumoured to be the owner of the madcap museum 'Ripley's Believe It Or Not'.

(◈)) The early Wurlitzer jukeboxes came with the following advertising spiel attached to the glass top by a large moulded plaque: 'The Wurlitzer has a panoramic sky top, built like a bomber's nose, which gives everyone a ringside seat as the record-changer mechanism works its magic in a dramatic, theatrical setting, right before their very eyes.' The reference to the 'bomber' relates to the fact that many early Wurlitzers were bought by US forces stationed at bases in the UK.

(◈)) Benjamin Britten's church opera *Curlew River* is based on a traditional Japanese Noh play.

(◈)) The pre-Christian instrument the *auloi*, a pair of reed pipes, was attached to the player's face with a tight cloth rope that went around the back of the head, thus exerting pressure on the cheeks and helping in the blowing of the reed.

(◈)) An instrument's string vibrates along its entire length, as well as in fractions of its length. The resulting harmonics are called 'upper partials' or overtones.

(◈)) Robert Fludd, the seventeenth-century astrologer, drew analogies between the theory of pitch and harmony and the mathematics behind architecture.

(((•))) 'This is a chord... this is another... this is a third. Now form a band.'
Message in the early punk fanzine *Sniffin' Glue*, next to crude diagrams of chord notation.

(((•))) Although associated with punk, albeit perhaps at its fringes, Tom Verlaine and Richard Lloyd of Television and Richard Hell of the Voidoids are acknowledged in classical guitar circles as virtuoso players.

(((•))) Eddie Van Halen is arguably the most technically gifted of all the modern metal guitarists. Take this explanation of the opening bars of the track 'Eruption' as taken from *The Cambridge Companion to the Guitar*: 'The A power chord that opens the track sets the harmonic centre around which Van Halen spins single-note lines of dazzling speed and intricacy; a predominantly pentatonic opening section, marked by muted picking and an array of hammer-ons and pull-offs, is capped by a wildly altered depression of the low E string with Van Halen's vibrato bar, which leads to a similarly wild vibrato-bar-driven ascent on the open A.' So is that a good review, then? Notably, this track was released in 1978, the same year that The Sex Pistols' guitarist Steve Jones said, 'I'd wake up in the morning, take a black beauty, play along with Iggy Pop and The New York Dolls' first album, throw in a little bit of Chuck Berry and that was it.'

(((•))) In 1985, The Kronos Quartet transformed Jimi Hendrix's signature tune 'Purple Haze' into a scored composition for a string quartet. Other musical transcribers claim parts of Hendrix's work are impossible to write down.

(((•))) Gram Parsons was said to have told his road manager that he wanted to be cremated at Joshua Tree National Monument in the event of his death; when he did die of an alcohol and morphine over-dose, his body was taken from LA Airport by the road manager and a colleague and duly burned at Joshua Tree.

((•)) After initially being seen among high society as a crude instrument, the violin boomed in popularity when travelling musicians and itinerant communities found the combination of its portability and wide range of sounds very appealing.

((•)) It is widely acknowledged that the very first piano was built by Bartolomeo Cristofori in Florence in the early 1700s and named as an abbreviation of *pianoforte* (from soft – *piano* – and loud – *forte*).

((•)) The great piano manufacturers Steinway were originally called Steinweg.

((•)) The first fully upright piano was introduced in London by its creator Robert Worum. Its design was partly inspired by the need to fit the piano into a domestic setting as both an instrument and a piece of furniture.

((•)) After pouring paint over their former record boss, his Mercedes, his girlfriend and his office in 1990, the four members of The Stone Roses were each fined £3,000.

((•)) During the first Gulf War, some DJs began to alter the words to songs to make their own unofficial comments on the conflict: songs changed included Milli Vanilli's 'Blame it on Hussein' ('Blame it on the Rain'), and the Fine Young Cannibals' 'Hussein is Crazy' ('She Drives me Crazy').

((•)) After Sinead O'Connor asked for 'The Star Spangled Banner' not to be played before one of her US shows in 1990, the outraged American media instilled her as Public Enemy Number 1 overnight. Some DJs even smashed her records on air.

((•)) The epic fifteen-minute rap single 'Rapper's Delight', the first song of that genre to sell in substantial quantities (in 1979), was nevertheless seen by most commentators as a one-off. By the late 90s, rap and hip hop were the most dominant commercial music genres in the world.

((•)) Joe Tex, Isaac Hayes, Millie Jackson and even Barry White had all used lengthy spoken-word sections, sometimes called 'rapping' in reviews, on their records back in the 60s and 70s.

((•)) The first Grammy for rap was awarded in 1989.

((•)) Rap's first two-million-selling single was Tone Loc's 'Wild Thing'.

((•)) Among the unlikely supporters of controversial rappers 2 Live Crew's million-selling-album *As Nasty as We Want to Be* were David Bowie and Bruce Springsteen. Bowie even interrupted his own show in Philadelphia in August 1990 to insist that their right to free speech should remain non-negotiable.

((•)) In the opening episode of MTV's most successful ever show, *The Osbournes*, the f-word bleeper is used sixty times.

((•)) Controversial but brilliant pop star Pink often wears a T-shirt during live shows that reads, 'Don't Bite me You Fucking Bitch or I'll Knock your Ass into next Week'. Her real name is Alecia Moore – not that you would want to ask.

Bibliography

Sources by other authors

Roberts, D (Ed.), *British Hit Singles*, Guinness, 2002.
Rees, D and Crampton, L, *Q Rock Stars Encyclopedia*, Dorling Kindersley, 1996.
Harry, B, *Whatever Happened To?*, Blandford, 1999.
Strong, MC, *The Great Rock Discography*, Canongate, 2002.
Rees, D and Crampton, L, *Rock and Pop Year by Year*, Dorling Kindersley, 2003.
Skinner, Q, *Casualties of Rock*, Pocket Books, 2001.
Gregory, H, *A Century of Pop*, Hamlyn, 1998.
Blackwood, A, *Music of the World*, Quarto Publishing, 1991
Coelho, VA (Ed.), *The Cambridge Companion to the Guitar*, Cambridge University Press, 2003.
Tibballs, G, *The Ultimate Lists Book*, Carlton, 1998.
Marsh, D and Bernard, J, *The New Book of Rock Lists*, Sidgwick & Jackson, 1994.
Kurtti, J, *The Great Movie Musical Trivia Book*, Applause Books, 1996.
Pickering, D, *The Cassell Companion to 20th Century Music*, Cassell, 1998.
Brown, T, Kutner, J and Warwick, N, *The Complete Book of the British Charts*, Omnibus Press, 2000.
Farren, M, *The Hitchhiker's Guide to Elvis*, The Book Press, 1996.
Tobler, J (Ed.), *The NME Rock 'n' Roll Years*, Hamlyn, 1991.
Calcutt, A, *Brit Cult*, Contemporary Books, 2000.
McAleer, D, *The All Music Book of Hit Albums*, Miller Freeman Books, 1995.
Savage, J, *England's Dreaming*, Faber & Faber, 2000.
Mann, W, *James Galway's Music in Time*, Mitchell Beazley, 1982.

Daly, S and Wice, N, *Alt.Culture*, Guardian Books, 1995.

Jasper, T, *The Top 20 Book*, Blandford Books, 1987.

Jones, D, *Haircults*, Thames and Hudson, 1990.

Obstfeld, R and Fitzgerald, P, *Jabberrock*, Canongate, 1997.

Dellio, P and Woods, S, *Quotable Pop*, Quotable Books, 2001.

McAleer, D, *The All Music Book of Hit Singles*, Miller Freeman Books, 1996.

Hindley, G, *The Larousse Encyclopedia of Music*, Hamlyn, 1976.

Polhemus, T, *Street Style*, Thames and Hudson, 1995.

Sources published by the author at Independent Music Press (IMP)

Brown, G, *Scooter Boys*, IMP, 2001.

Watson, G, *Skins*, IMP, 2001.

James, M, *Moby – Replay*, IMP, 1999.

Black, M, *Stereophonics*, IMP, 1999.

Charles, G, *Bikers*, IMP, 2003.

James, M, *Dave Grohl*, IMP, 2003.

Eddington, R, *Sent from Coventry: the Chequered Past of Two Tone*, IMP, 2004.

Weird & Gilly, *Mick Ronson*, IMP, 2002.

Myers, B, *Muse*, IMP, 2004.

Sources by the author

NME Top 100 Singles, Chrysalis Impact Books, 2002.

Dr Martens – the Story of an Icon, Chrysalis Impact Books, 2003.

The White Stripes and the Strange Relevance of Detroit, Chrome Dreams, 2004.

So You Want to be a Pop Star, Virgin, 2003.

The Strokes, Omnibus Press, 2003.

Justin Timberlake, Virgin, 2003.

The Red Hot Chili Peppers, Chrome Dreams, 2004.

MISCELLANEOUS SOURCES

MAGAZINES AND NEWSPAPERS

Q, *Nuts*, *Loaded*, the *Sunday Times*, the *Daily Telegraph*, the *Belfast Telegraph*, *Sunday magazine*, the *Sun*, the *Daily Mirror*, *News of the World*, The Associated Press, Teletext, Ceefax.

WEBSITES

http://www.bbc.co.uk
http://www.faqs.org/faqs/music/hip-hop/dictionary/part1/
http://www.rapdict.org
http://www.the smokinggun.com/backstagetour/
http://www.mtsu.edu/~smpte/pre20s.html
www.Deadrockstarsweb.com